Lord of the Saved

Lord of the Saved

Getting to the Heart of the Lordship Debate

KENNETH L. GENTRY, JR.

P&R

PUBLISHING

P.O. BOX 817 • PHILLIPSBURG • NEW JERSEY 08865-0817

Unless otherwise indicated, Scripture quotations are from The Holy Bible, New King James Version, copyright © 1979, 1980, 1982 by Thomas Nelson, Inc., Nashville, Tennessee. Italic in Scripture quotations represents the author's emphasis.

Manufactured in the United States of America

Library of Congress Cataloging-in-Publication Data

Gentry, Kenneth L.
    Lord of the saved : getting to the heart of the Lordship debate / Kenneth L. Gentry.
       p.   cm.
    Includes bibliographical references and index.
    ISBN 0-87552-265-3
    1. Salvation. 2. Jesus Christ—Lordship. 3. Christian life.
I. Title.
BT752.G46 1992
232'.8—dc20   92-24057

Contents

Preface

This book is an expanded and updated version of a lengthy article I wrote in 1976, entitled, "The Great Option: A Study of the Lordship Controversy."[1] At the time, the debate over lordship salvation was very much alive, but contained. Like a flickering flame it sporadically flared up in the works of scattered authors. Today, owing largely to John F. MacArthur's *The Gospel According to Jesus* (1988), the issue has become a raging inferno. *Christianity Today* has called it a "volcanic issue."[2] Robert Lightner surmises that "at the present time 'Lordship Salvation' is probably the most disputed concept about the Savior and His salvation among evangelicals."[3]

MacArthur reports that in the first two years of its publication, he received thousands of letters regarding his book.[4] Because of the firestorm of controversy and debate it ignited, *The Gospel According to Jesus* was widely reviewed in such periodicals as *Alliance Life* (4 Jan. 1989), *Bibliotheca Sacra* (Jan.–Mar. 1989), *Grace Theological Jour-*

nal (Spring 1989), *Biblical Viewpoint* (Apr. 1989), *Criswell Theological Review* (Fall 1989), *Fundamentalist Journal* (Mar. 1989), *Andrews University Seminary Studies* (Spring 1990), *Southwestern Theological Journal* (Fall 1990), *Moody Monthly* (Nov. 1990), and others.

The most notable books written in rebuttal to MacArthur's work include: Zane Hodges's *Absolutely Free! A Biblical Reply to Lordship Salvation* (1989), Charles C. Ryrie's *So Great Salvation: What It Means to Believe in Jesus Christ* (1989), and Robert P. Lightner's *Sin, the Savior, and Salvation: The Theology of Everlasting Life* (1991). Some of the significant periodicals highlighting the topic and giving strong emphasis to the book include the following: *Bibliotheca Sacra* published scattered articles related to the debate (1989–91); *The Journal of the Evangelical Theological Society* published contributions by MacArthur and responses by E. D. Radmacher and Robert L. Saucy (1990); *Christianity Today* provided a five-page assessment of the issues involved in the controversy (1989); *Southwestern Journal of Theology* (1991) gave almost a total issue to matters surrounding the debate.[5]

Of course, the issue was not created by MacArthur—and it will not die with him. In fact, Lightner observes that lordship doctrine is "as old as covenant reformed theology." MacArthur, more accurately, traces it through ancient church history to the apostles.[6] Yet, as I have mentioned, the doctrine is flaring up even more brightly today. It is probably safe to say that "the forerunner of the current debate erupted in the late 1950s and early 1960s" when "two well-known evangelicals, Everett F. Harrison and John R. W. Stott, debated the issue in *Eternity* magazine in September 1959."[7]

Following the 1959 *Eternity* debate, the issue began cropping up much more frequently in evangelical writings. We see it in such pre-MacArthur theological contributions as J. I. Packer's *Evangelism and the Sovereignty of God* (1961), Charles C. Ryrie's *Balancing the Christian Life* (1969), Walter Chantry's *Today's Gospel: Authentic or Synthetic?* (1970), Zane Hodges's *The Gospel Under Siege* (1981), G. M. Cocoris's *Lordship Salvation: Is It Biblical?* (1983) and *Evangelism: A Biblical Approach* (1984), Zane Hodges's *Grace in Eclipse* (1985) and *Dead Faith: What Is It?* (1987), and James Montgomery Boice's *Christ's Call to Discipleship* (1986), to name but a few from both sides of the issue.[8]

That the debate was alive and the issue deemed important before MacArthur's book, became evident to me in my own experience with my original 1976 article. Over the years since its publication, I have received numerous requests for the article from those who have seen either the original or references to it in other works. In fact in 1977 the article was even copied and distributed throughout the Evangelical Free Church by Rev. Roy C. Anderson. I have been pleasantly surprised that the original article still receives attention at this late date.

Though written for a class during my second year at Grace Theological Seminary, it apparently focused on the issues succinctly enough to prove helpful to others. Reference to it has been found in a number of works, most notably MacArthur's *The Gospel According to Jesus* (1988), which recommended the article for its "excellent lexical analysis of the New Testament usage" of the word "Lord."[9] Those opposed to lordship salvation found it a useful tool as well; see especially Charles Ryrie's *Basic Theology* (1986) and *So Great Salvation* (1989) and Robert P. Lightner's *Sin, the Savior, and Salvation* (1991).[10]

Two events finally led me to seek its republication in the present updated and slightly expanded form. One of these was a two-hour debate in 1990 on WMUZ radio in Detroit with J. Kevin Butcher. Butcher is a nonlordship advocate, disciple of Zane Hodges, and contributor to the *Journal of the Grace Evangelical Society.* The debate generated enough radio call-ins and correspondence to suggest that the article might be helpful in the current context.

The second event was its review almost fifteen years after its original publication in the *Journal of the Grace Evangelical Society.* This journal was established as the publication arm of the Grace Evangelical Society, which has as its express purpose the defense of the nonlordship view of salvation. "The Grace Evangelical Society was formed 'to promote the clear proclamation of God's free salvation through faith alone in Christ alone, which is properly correlated with and distinguished from issues related to discipleship.'"[11]

Though obviously disagreeing with the position taken in my article, the reviewer noted: "This older article merits review because it is a classic statement and defense of the Lordship Salvation position. It has done much to shape subsequent Lordship presentations and free grace responses. . . . What is most commendable about Gentry's work is its clear and logical organization. . . . here is as clear and concise a statement of the position as can be found anywhere." The reviewer went on to "recommend this article to all who want a succinct explanation of the Lordship Salvation position by a confirmed Lordship Salvationist. It will help define the crux of the debate and hopefully stir the reader to seek and refine answers to the most frequent and formidable Lordship arguments."[12]

I greatly appreciate Presbyterian and Reformed Publishing Company's willingness to publish the study in its present expanded form. Much of my early theological development was fed by publications from Presbyterian and Reformed, and I still look to them for theological sustenance.

I pray that this small book might be helpful in this important debate and that it would encourage a greater fear of God among those who would preach the gospel in its purity.

Notes

1. Kenneth L. Gentry, Jr., "The Great Option: A Study of the Lordship Controversy," *Baptist Reformation Review* 5 (Spring 1976): 49–79.

2. S. Lewis Johnson, "How Faith Works," *Christianity Today*, 22 Sept. 1989, 21.

3. Robert P. Lightner, *The Savior, Sin, and Salvation* (Nashville: Nelson, 1991), 200.

4. John F. MacArthur, Jr., Earl D. Radmacher, and Robert L. Saucy "Faith According to the Apostle James," *Journal of the Evangelical Theological Society* 33 (March 1990): 13.

5. MacArthur, Radmacher, and Saucy, "Faith According to the Apostle James," 13–34, 35–41, 43–47; *Bibliotheca Sacra*, nos. 585–92; *Southwestern Theological Journal* 33 (Spring 1991).

6. Lightner, *Savior, Sin, and Salvation,* 203; John F. MacArthur, *The Gospel According to Jesus* (Grand Rapids: Zondervan, 1988), appendix 2. In an article admitting its antiquity, Thomas G. Lewellen discounts the value of church history: "Has Lordship Salvation Been Taught throughout Church History?" *Bibliotheca Sacra* 585 (Jan.–Mar. 1990): 54–68.

7. Johnson, "How Faith Works," 21–25. See John R. W. Stott, "Must Christ Be Lord to Be Savior—Yes!" and Everett F. Harrison, "Must Christ Be Lord to Be Savior—No!" in *Eternity* 10 (Sept. 1959): 13ff.

8. J. I. Packer, *Evangelism and the Sovereignty of God* (London: InterVarsity, 1961); Charles C. Ryrie, *Balancing the Christian Life* (Chicago: Moody, 1969); Walter Chantry, *Today's Gospel: Authentic or Synthetic?* (Carlisle, Pa.: Banner of Truth, 1970); G. M. Cocoris, *Lordship Salvation: Is It Biblical?* (Dallas: Redencion Viva, 1983) and *Evangelism: A Biblical Approach* (Chicago: Moody, 1984); Zane C. Hodges, *The Gospel Under Siege* (Dallas: Redencion Viva, 1981), *Grace in Eclipse* (Dallas: Redencion Viva, 1985), and *Dead Faith: What Is It?* (Dallas: Redencion Viva, 1987); James Montgomery Boice, *Christ's Call to Discipleship* (Chicago: Moody, 1986).

9. MacArthur, *Gospel According to Jesus,* 206.

10. Charles C. Ryrie, *Basic Theology* (Wheaton, Ill.: Victor, 1986), 338 and *So Great Salvation* (Wheaton, Ill: Victor, 1989), 107. Lightner, *Sin, the Savior, and Salvation,* 202.

11. Statement of purpose, *Journal of the Grace Evangelical Society* 3 (Spring 1989): 2. The editor is Arthur L. Farstad. Zane C. Hodges is one of its listed associate editors.

12. Charles C. Bing, "Periodical Reviews," *The Journal of the Grace Evangelical Society* 3 (Spring 1990): 93, 94.

1

The Debate Unfolds

Enter by the narrow gate; for wide is the gate and broad is the way that leads to destruction, and there are many who go in by it. Because narrow is the gate and difficult is the way which leads to life, and there are few who find it. (Matt. 7:13–14)

The Problem

The Christian church established by Jesus Christ nearly two thousand years ago is very much alive and growing today. The tremendous expansion of Christendom from Pentecost to the present is exemplified by the fact that the population of "professing" believers within the church has reached 1,711,897,000, or nearly one–third of the population of the world.[1] As is recognized by many news reports, there is much growth occurring still today.[2] The ranks of those in

America claiming to be "born again" has steadily climbed from 35 percent of adults in 1978 to 38 percent in 1988.[3]

The growth of Christianity is certainly a source of exultation for the true child of God, for he longs to see his Master's truth advanced and sinners saved. But the statistics as reported by the *World Almanac, World Christian Handbook*, and other sources may differ widely from those actually inscribed in the Lamb's Book of Life (Rev. 21:27).

Even when manifestly false Christian churches, aberrant movements, and heretical cults are deleted from the polls, the figures are suspect. Sadly, within the evangelical churches of America there are a large number of unregenerate professing believers. That is evidenced by the moral and spiritual conditions of many within these churches and the carnal, meaningless goals of the church leaders themselves.[4]

Large scale "revivals" and evangelistic campaigns frequently result in thousands responding to the message preached. Yet even when the one proclaiming the message is an earnest Christian, the respondents too often prove to be only temporary converts moved by emotion rather than the Spirit. Many soon lapse back into their former manner of living. Or worse yet, they remain in the churches, swelling the membership roles and infiltrating positions of leadership, thereby compounding the problem.

This book will deal with the doctrinal implications of Jesus' lordship, as contrasted to the pervasive "easy believism" that is so rampant today. The basic issue in the "lordship controversy," as MacArthur observes, has to do with "what Scripture means when it speaks of faith."[5] It is my hope that the reader will become aware of some of the real dangers of preaching "simply believe" to vast multitudes who are living in various degrees of sinfulness, who know nothing of the demands of the gospel, and who care nothing for the "straight and narrow way." The problem with the modern presentation of Christ is deadly serious and needs to be squarely faced.

Method of Approach

The purpose of this book is that the gospel of the Lord Jesus Christ be properly and faithfully preached to a world of lost sinners. My concern is that an improper, shallow presentation of the gospel is driving many to a merely psychological or emotional conversion. God can and surely does use all preaching for a purpose (even improperly motivated preaching—Phil. 1:15–18). And though He could raise up stones to proclaim Christ (Luke 19:40), it is the responsibility of His children to present Christ as scripturally and clearly as possible.

The often simplistic methods employed in our time are dangerous. Arthur Pink warned of the danger, when he wrote, "A promise misapplied will be *a seal upon the sepulchre*, making them sure in the grave of sin, wherein they lay dead and rotting."[6]

This book is not written to condemn anyone. Rather, it is a brief examination of the serious problems inherent in the shallow preaching of the gospel today. The main question is whether Jesus Christ can be accepted

3

as Savior simply, as the "faith only" or "free grace" advocates argue. Or whether He can be truly realized as Savior only when He is acknowledged as *Lord* in the act of faith, as lordship advocates teach. The perspective presented in the following pages is that of lordship advocacy.

Often straw men are burned in effigy as lordship doctrine is mistakenly associated with the nonscriptural doctrines of perfectionism and works salvation. A proper understanding of the system, however, demonstrates that such straw men are not the "representation of the reality," to borrow a notion from Hebrews 1:3. All "lordship" spokesmen cited within this study teach the scriptural doctrine of *justification through faith apart from meritorious works.* The various elements they emphasize that are often erroneously labeled as works oriented are simply components of the total message of salvation. Although the lordship debate is often obscured by "occasionally fuzzy, sometimes inept, and even theologically inaccurate" terminology,[7] the real problem is not merely semantical and technical, but theological and practical.

In these pages I will first give a brief analysis of the two viewpoints in the lordship controversy. Following that I will seek to demonstrate the validity of the lordship stance by exploring four vital areas of concern.

Two Basic Views

There are within evangelical circles several views of salvation relative to the lordship issue. But basically these may all be boiled down to two fundamental types: the nonlordship and the lordship views. Though differences exist within these camps as to the meaning of sanctification and other related doctrines, the basic question under scrutiny is simply, *Must Christ be accepted as Lord in order to be truly one's Savior?* To answer yes to this question puts one in the lordship camp; to answer no makes one a nonlordship advocate.

The Nonlordship View

The nonlordship view of the gospel message is by far the more popular one in American evangelicalism today. Such a comment may surprise some adherents to the nonlordship view.[8] But it is doubtful whether the tremendous strides in the church growth movement are lordship gains. Indeed, the popularity of nonlordship commitments is evidenced by the prevalence of books on related subjects by writers or ministries such as L. S. Chafer, Theodore Epp, Zane Hodges, Hal Lindsey, Ruth Paxson, J. Dwight Pentecost, Charles C. Ryrie, R. B. Thieme, Robert Lightner, Warren W. Wiersbe, Roy B. Zuck, Campus Crusade for Christ, and others. Its influence is heightened by its incorporation into popular study Bibles such as the *Scofield Reference Bible*, the *New Scofield Reference Bible*, and the *Ryrie Study Bible*.

In the recently renewed debate there has even been the establishment of a journal devoted to nonlordship argumentation, increasingly called the "free grace" position: *The Journal of the Grace Evangelical Society*. I will not use the label "free grace" to designate the nonlordship position because it wrongly suggests that the lordship view denies the freeness of God's grace.

Below are several pertinent quotes from the main proponents of the nonlordship view. I quote these passages to demonstrate the flow of thought on this particular doctrine, not to represent its entire theological framework.

Charles Ryrie certainly brings the point of contention to the fore in his *Balancing the Christian Life*, when he states:

> The importance of this question cannot be overestimated in relation to both salvation and sanctification. The message of faith only and the message of faith plus commitment of life cannot both be the gospel; therefore, one of them is false and comes under the curse of perverting the gospel or preaching another gospel (Gal. 1:6–9). . . .[9]

Lightner agrees: "These views—the absolutely free gift view and the lordship view—cannot both be right. They are mutually exclusive."[10] Both Ryrie and Lightner are correct in assessing the differences between the two views as being serious. Ryrie's accusation is especially bold, necessitating the clarification of the lordship doctrine.

L. S. Chafer states with amazing candor the side-effects of the nonlordship view: "The Christian's liberty *to do precisely as he chooses* is as limitless and perfect as any other aspect of grace."[11] Thus the practical issues in the debate come into clear focus.

Likewise Zane C. Hodges writes: "Saving faith is taking God at His Word in the gospel. It is nothing less than this. But it is also nothing more." Regarding God's loving call to salvation, "God's love can embrace sinful people unconditionally, with no binding requirements attached at all."[12] Salvation, he argues, involves "no spiritual commitment whatsoever."[13]

Reflecting the severity of the problem, Chafer refers to "the great mass of carnal Christians," and Ryrie worries about lordship advocacy by questioning, "Where is there room for carnal Christians?"[14] No doubt lordship adherents would regard many "carnal Christians" to be false converts, who have only an inadequate knowledge of the truth at best. Hodges admits, "To be sure, there is much reason to think that there are multitudes of people in churches today who have never really been saved."[15]

This "great mass of carnal Christians" is the subject of many books on Christian living. Broadly speaking there are two dominant viewpoints within the nonlordship camp as to how to understand these people. One is the "discipleship" view, represented by Ryrie, Chafer, and Hodges. The other is designated the "Higher Life" or "Victorious Life" movement. Both agree to a large extent on the life of the carnal Christian. Their basic difference lies in their understandings of how one moves from the "carnal status" to the "spiritual status."[16]

Ruth Paxson represents the Higher Life segment of the nonlordship camp. Her views of the walk of the "carnal Christian" (a regenerate person living in opposition to Christ) are identical to those of the discipleship view. She speaks of the carnal walk of the Christian as "a life of adulterous infidelity" exemplified in "dishonoring hypocrisy."[17] While obviously relevant to the doctrine of sanctification, such statements are also vitally related to the lordship issue. They raise the question, Is a Christian out from under Christ's controlling authority until he himself decides to live wholly for Christ? Paxson answers in the affirmative: "By a definite, voluntary act of the will the believer must choose Christ as his new Master and yield himself to Him as Lord."[18]

Thus, the nonlordship persuasion emphatically teaches that it is not necessary to commit one's life to Christ in the act of receiving Him as Savior. This is the crux of the problem. Later we shall examine in greater detail the reasoning and Scripture used to support this position.

The Lordship View

Lordship doctrine has fallen upon hard times, having been largely forgotten by the majority of evangelical churches. It has been espoused, however, by such noteworthy scholars as Emery Bancroft, Louis Berkhof, James M. Boice, John H. Gerstner, Homer A. Kent, R. B. Kuiper, John F. MacArthur, Jr., John Murray, J. I. Packer, A. W. Pink, R. C. Sproul, John R. W. Stott, and Henry Theissen. It is largely associated with Reformed or Calvinistic theology, though not exclusively, for Kent, MacArthur, and Theissen are dispensationalists.

MacArthur admits that doctrinal elements within dispensationalism generally predispose one to non-lordship commitments.[19] That seems at least partially related to dispensationalism's understanding of God's covenants in Scripture as wholly unconditional, and therefore without covenantal obligations.[20] Concerning the Reformed view of covenantal obedience Hodges complains: "In the English-speaking world, this radically altered concept of saving faith can with considerable fairness be described as Puritan theology. Lordship salvation in its best known contemporary form, simply popularizes the Puritanism to which it is heir."[21] Lightner and Gerstner note its strong Reformed connections, as well.[22]

The lordship view has largely suffered, not from its connection with Calvinism, but from its misrepresentation by Arminian and Pelagian writers. Many have erroneously charged lordship proponents with teaching that works are prerequisite, meritorious efforts on the part of the sinner. On the contrary, lordship adherents consistently teach salvation by grace through faith. It must always be dogmatically affirmed that works *never* merit salvation!

John Stott clearly sums up the issue when he writes, "The astonishing idea is current in some circles today that we can enjoy the benefits of Christ's salvation without accepting the challenge of His sovereign Lordship."[23] This is in vivid contrast to Ryrie's statement quoted above.

In his characteristically frank manner, A. W. Pink illustrates the problem by warning:

> In most instances the modern "evangelist" assures his congregation that *all* any sinner has to do in order to escape Hell and make sure of Heaven is to "receive Christ as his personal Saviour." But such teaching is utterly misleading. No one can receive Christ as His Saviour while he *rejects Him as Lord*. . . . Therefore,

those who have not bowed to Christ's scepter and enthroned Him in their hearts and lives, and yet imagine that they are trusting Him as Saviour, *are deceived. . . .*[24]

The lordship view expressly states the need to acknowledge Christ as the Lord and Master of one's life in the act of truly receiving Him as Savior. These are not two different, sequential acts (or successive steps), but rather one act of pure, trusting faith. It takes little theological acumen to discern the vast differences between the lordship and nonlordship views of the presentation of the gospel.

At the same time, lordship advocacy fully endorses the Reformation principle of salvation by grace through faith. "The question is not whether good works are necessary to salvation, but in what way are they necessary. As the inevitable outworking of saving faith, they are necessary for salvation. As the meritorious ground of justification, they are not necessary *or acceptable.*"[25]

Conclusion

When two positions disagree so unreservedly, it is one thing. But when that disagreement involves the doctrine of salvation, the debate takes on a new dimension. The two views are as opposite as black and white, as incompatible as oil and water, a fact noted by contributors on both sides of the debate. Both camps are decidedly evangelical and convinced their positions are grounded in Scripture. Therefore, it is not a question of philosophical presuppositions set in defiance to scriptural revelation. The polarity of opinion is an interpretive problem concerned primarily with the proper understanding of the gospel message.

Four issues in the controversy must be clarified. These issues concern the nature of and relationships between faith, repentance, Christ's lordship, and discipleship. Of course, other issues are involved, but these are the leading ones. I will survey these vital matters in the remainder of the book.

Notes

1. *World Almanac and Book of Facts 1991* (New York: World Almanac, 1991), 610.

2. Recent articles in *Christianity Today*, alone evidence this fact: "Protestant Growth," *Christianity Today*, 25 Nov. 1991, 56. Ken Sidey, "Church Growth Fine Tunes Its Formulas, "*Christianity Today*, 24 June 1991, 44ff. "Ranks of 'Born Again' Grow," *Christianity Today*, 14 Jan. 1991, 64. "World's Largest," *Christianity Today*, 11 March 1991, 72. Lyle Schaller, "Megachurch!," *Christianity Today*, 5 March 1990, 20ff.

3. "Ranks of 'Born Again' Grow," 64.

4. The most tragic illustration of the problem is documented in Michael Horton, ed., *The Agony of Deceit: What Some TV Preachers Are Really Preaching* (Chicago: Moody, 1990).

5. John F. MacArthur, Jr., Earl D. Radmacher, and Robert L. Saucy, "Faith According to the Apostle James," *Journal of the Evangelical Theological Society* 33 (March 1990): 13. J. I. Packer agrees in his foreword to MacArthur's *The Gospel According to Jesus*.

6. Arthur W. Pink, *Studies on Saving Faith* (Swengel, Pa.: Reiner, n.d.), 21.

7. S. Lewis Johnson, "How Faith Works," *Christianity Today*, 22 Sept. 1989, 21.

8. Charles C. Bing, "Periodical Reviews," *The Journal of the Grace Evangelical Society* 3 (Spring 1990): 93.

9. Charles C. Ryrie, *Balancing the Christian Life* (Chicago: Moody, 1969), 170.

10. Robert P. Lightner, *The Savior, Sin, and Salvation* (Nashville: Nelson, 1991), 200.

11. Lewis Sperry Chafer, *Grace: The Glorious Theme* (Grand Rapids: Zondervan, 1922, 1950), 345, emphasis mine. This work had gone through more than twenty-three printings by the 1980s.

12. Zane C. Hodges, *Absolutely Free! A Biblical Reply to Lordship Salvation* (Grand Rapids: Zondervan, 1989), 32, 49.

13. Zane C. Hodges, *The Gospel Under Siege* (Dallas: Redencion Viva, 1981), 14.

14. Chafer, *Grace*, 346. Ryrie, *Balancing the Christian Life*, 170.

15. Hodges, *Absolutely Free!*, 19.

16. The appendix should be consulted here, however. There are strong similarities at crucial points between the views. For an excellent and still relevant expose of the theological kinship of the "discipleship" and the "Higher Life" views, see Benjamin B. Warfield, "Review of *He That Is Spiritual*, by Lewis Sperry Chafer," *Princeton Theological Review* 17 (April 1919): 322–27.

17. Ruth Paxson, *Life on the Highest Plane* (Chicago: Bible Institute Colportage, 1941), 2:199.

18. Ibid., 123.

19. John F. MacArthur, Jr., *The Gospel According to Jesus* (Grand Rapids: Zondervan, 1988), xv, 25, 26, 89.

20. O. T. Allis, *Prophecy and the Church* (Philadelphia: Presbyterian and Reformed, 1945), 42–43. I write a monthly newsletter noting this and other problems inherent in dispensationalism, entitled "Dispensationalism in Transition."

To subscribe, write to: Institute for Christian Economics, P. O. Box 8000, Tyler, TX 75711.

21. Hodges, *Absolutely Free!*, 33.

22. Lightner, *Savior, Sin, and Salvation*, 203. John H. Gerstner, *Wrongly Dividing the Word of Truth: A Critique of Dispensationalism* (Brentwood, Tenn.: Wolgemuth & Hyatt, 1991), 213–30.

23. John R. W. Stott, *Basic Christianity* (Grand Rapids: Eerdmans, 1958), 114.

24. Pink, *Studies on Saving Faith*, 12–13.

25. Gerstner, *Wrongly Dividing the Word of Truth*, 210.

2

Faith and Salvation

*Now when He was in Jerusalem at the Passover,
during the feast, many believed in His name when
they saw the signs which He did. But Jesus did not
commit Himself to them, because He knew all men,
and had no need that anyone should testify of man,
for He knew what was in man. (John 2:23–25)*

The Problem

Many contemporary gospel presentations can be
summarized by the phrase "only believe." The concept
of faith in Christ often associated with "only believe"
preaching is sometimes termed "easy believism." Often
the facts of the crucifixion, burial, and resurrection of
the Lord receive brief mention before those hearing this
message are urged to "only believe." Hodges chastises
lordship advocates for requiring something more: "The
result is that what passes for faith in lordship thought

15

is no longer recognizable as the biblical quality that goes by the same name."[1] He is correct in focusing on the quality of faith as a key issue. Indeed the question is, What does biblical faith entail?

In response to the charge of "easy believism," Ryrie offers two reasons that belief is not easy: (1) Christ lived two thousand years ago and, therefore, cannot be seen today, and (2) this distant and unseen person must be trusted for one's eternal destiny.[2] Hodges adds: "The writers of Scripture knew perfectly well how hostile their environment was to the acceptance of Christian truth. . . . They recognized clearly how difficult that was for both Jew and Gentile alike."[3]

But these are not the real problem. The central problem is man's total depravity (Eph. 2:1–3; Rom. 3:10–19), his blindness to spiritual truth (1 Cor. 2:14; 2 Cor. 4:4), his natural enmity against God (Rom. 8:6–8; John 6:44). The difficulty of belief lies rooted in sin, not in location or intellect. Using Ryrie's logic it could be argued that belief in Christ was a relatively simple task in Christ's day when He could be seen, heard, and handled—and while He was performing wondrous miracles.

Belief in the biblical sense is not difficult—it is *impossible:* "No one can come to Me unless the Father who sent Me draws him; and I will raise him up at the last day" (John 6:44). Only by sovereign intervention and gracious initiative by God can a man believe in Christ, because we are spiritually "born, not of blood, nor of the will of the flesh, nor of the will of man, but of God" (John 1:13). "This is the work of God, that you believe in Him whom He sent" (John 6:29). Furthermore, given the credulity of the ancient pagan mind, with its "many

gods and many lords" (1 Cor. 8:5) and its ready acceptance of myth and legend, how would it be difficult to
believe that Jesus was God?

Generally speaking, the nonlordship proponents
present Christ as Savior to be accepted by faith that
is devoid of any idea of commitment to Him. The
average nonlordship churchman can often by heard
witnessing with such words as: "Give Jesus a chance."
"Suppose His claims are false, what have you lost?"
"Try God." "Let go and let God." Faith in Christ
tends to be little more than accepting the facts of His
deity and atonement apart from any idea of obeying
Him. Hodges writes:

> Over a period of many years the idea has gained
> ground that true saving faith is somehow distinguish-
> able from false kinds of faith, primarily by means of
> its results or "fruits."
>
> Thus two men might believe exactly the same
> things in terms of content, yet if one of them exhibited
> what seemed to be a "fruitless" Christian experience,
> his faith would be condemned as "intellectual assent,"
> or "head belief" over against "heart belief." In a word,
> his faith was false faith—it was faith that did not, and
> could not, save. . . .
>
> In every other sphere of life, except religion, we
> do not puzzle ourselves with introspective questions
> about the "nature" of our faith.[4]

To a large extent Hodges is correct about the difference between the lordship persuasion and his own. The
lordship view teaches that inextricably bound up in the
very idea of faith *in Christ* is the understanding that the
One believed in is to be trusted and obeyed.

The contrast between the two systems can be well illustrated by a quotation from a proponent of each side. Ryrie suggests that the believer is in a higher position of freedom than the unbeliever because: "The believer has an option. He may serve God, and as long as he is in a human body he may also choose to leave God out and live according to the old nature."[5] In stark contrast, Stott views the act of faith and the life resulting from it this way: Christ "does not call us to a sloppy half-heartedness, but to a vigorous, absolute commitment."[6] Certainly these are vastly different concepts of faith and the union with Christ in which one is placed by means of that faith. It is therefore important to know exactly what faith truly is.

Lexical Relationships

Figure 1 lists the Greek words bearing the concept of "faith" in the New Testament, their frequency of occurrence, and their translations in the King James Version. The words *pisteuo* and *pistos* are quite common and, therefore, are especially informative regarding the relationship of faith to salvation. In his lexical manual, Metzger lists ninety-six separate word groups. Each group shares a clear relationship in its base form. The arrangement of the selected word groups is based on scientific linguistic principles, thus assuring that the words within each group have firmly established historical-grammatical relation ships.

The *PITH*-Word Group

Part of speech	Greek word	Occurrences	KJV translations
Verb	*pisteuo*	247	believe, trust, commit
Verb	*peitho*	43	believe, trust, assure, be confident, persuade, yield
Noun	*pistis*	244	assurance, faith, belief
Adj.	*pistos*	66	believing, faithful, sure, true

Figure 1

The words in Figure 1 are from the group having as its base the root stem *pith,* which carries the sense "to bind."[7] The idea of "binding" has a dominant influence on the concept of faith and is of great significance to the lordship controversy.

The Baur-Arndt-Gingrich *Lexicon* renders the noun *pistis* as involving "trust, confidence."[8] Of its verbal form *pisteuo,* Vine explains, "To believe, also to be persuaded of, and hence, to place confidence in, to trust, signifies, in this sense of the word, reliance upon, not mere credence."[9] What kind of trust or reliance is it that does not obey? To trust Jesus Christ, the Lord of the universe, must involve submission to Him as Lord and Master of one's life. *A person cannot be relying on Christ if he chooses to chart his own life course in opposition to Christ from the very outset of his faith relationship.*

As the *Theological Dictionary of the New Testament* well notes, "In as much as trust may be a duty, *pistos* can come to have the nuance of 'obedient.'"[10] It correlates the relationship of New Testament faith with that of the Old Testament, showing that both revolve around obedience. This, the dictionary notes, is particularly emphasized in the great chapter of faith, Hebrews 11.[11] In each of the examples in "the hall of faith" in Hebrews 11 there is the *obedient action* of faith.

Faith is clearly related to obedience (Greek: *hupakoe*) in Pauline theology. Faith to Paul is "obey[ing] the gospel" (*hupokouein to euaggelio*, Rom. 10:16; cp. 2 Thess. 1:7–8). Paul praises the Roman church at the outset of his epistle because its "faith is spoken of throughout the whole world" (Rom. 1:8). At the close of Romans he associates faith with obedience by expressing the same thought in other words: "Your obedience has become known to all" (Rom. 16:19). He even says in 1 Corinthians 1:17 that his ministry is "to preach the gospel," whereas in Romans 15:18 he says it is "to make the Gentiles obedient." In short, Paul speaks freely of obedient faith as being the way of salvation (Rom. 1:5; 6:17; 16:26; cp. Acts 6:7; Heb. 11:8). Thus, faith binds a man in trusting obedience to Christ the Lord.

In Hebrews 5:9 we read that Jesus "became the author of eternal salvation unto all who obey Him." As Stott well states, "The bended knee is as much a part of saving faith as the open hand."[12] Christ is the Christian's Master. When one believes in Christ, he is bound to Him in an obedient, vital relationship. Commitment is an essential element in the act of believing. Faith is not merely intellectual assent.

Prepositional Relationships

The connection between faith and obedient submission to Christ can further be seen in the grammatical relationships in which *pisteuo* occurs in the New Testament. To the Greek-oriented mind the idea of "believe" could have two connotations, each expressed by a distinct grammatical structure. To believe a person was one thing, but to believe *in* or *on* a person was quite another.

The prepositions *eis* ("into"), *epi* ("upon"), and *en* ("in") make a remarkable difference in meaning when used in association with *pisteuo*. Figure 2 lists the types of relationship and their number of occurrences in the New Testament.

Prepositional Relationships of "Faith"

Preposition	Case of Object	Occurrences Believed	Examples
epi	Dative	5	1 Tim. 1:16
epi	Accusative	7	Acts 16:31
eis	Accusative	49	Gal. 2:16
en	Dative	1*	Mark 1:15

*Common in the Greek translation of the Old Testament, but superseded by *eis* + accusative in the New Testament

Figure 2

The difference can be traced to Classical Greek usage and is well illustrated by Moulton:

21

In classical Greek, as LS observe "the two notions [*believe* and *believe in*] run into each other." To be unable to distinguish ideas so vitally different in the scheme of Christianity would certainly have been a serious matter for the NT writers.

To repose one's trust *upon* God or Christ was well expressed by *pisteuein epi*, the dative suggesting more of the state, and the accusative more of the initial act of faith; while *eis* recalls at once the bringing of the soul *into* that mystical union which Paul loved to express by *en Christo*. But as between *epi* and *eis*, we may freely admit that it is not safe to refine too much: the difference may amount to little more than that between our own *believe on* and *believe in*. The really important matter is the recognition of a clear distinction between *believe on* or *in* and *believe* with the dative simply.[13]

A. T. Robertson, as well as most other noted Greek grammarians, agrees. He too notes the significance of a proper understanding of the case relationships: "It is essential that one look at the Greek cases historically and from the Greek point of view. Foreigners may not appreciate all the niceties, but they can understand the respective import of the Greek cases."[14]

Thus, for a Greek-speaking person to say that he believed "into" someone (*eis* plus the accusative), or "upon" someone (*epi* plus the accusative or dative) was a strong statement. The effect was that he was placing his entire confidence, trust, or hope *into* that person or grounding it *upon* his character as revealed to him. Such faith entailed full confidence in the character, claims, and authority of that person. The very act of placing faith into Christ must imply submission to Him—or else it could not be said that one's trust rested fully "in Christ." As mentioned earlier, Christ is God, and therefore His authority is supreme. Knowing this, the person coming to Him must certainly recognize his own humanity, finiteness, and sinfulness, and must be willing to subject his will to Christ's at the moment he trusts in Him. What trust is it that distrusts at the outset?

Many people may claim to believe Christ (in the sense of *pisteuo* plus the dative case without a preposition), but this is a far cry from truly placing one's trust wholly *in* Him.

> The gospel, or message of salvation, which is offered to faith is more than a discourse concerning Christ. It is an actual presentation of Christ, a definite offer of Christ. . . . The due response to the message, therefore, cannot be merely an intellectual assent to the propositions it contains regarding Christ. . . . It must consist in hearty consent to the claims made on behalf of Christ, which indeed he makes for himself—an owning of Christ, in an individual act of homage, as supreme in the whole realm of human life; a personal acceptance of Him as Savior and Lord. . . .[15]

Christ as a whole person—Lord and Savior—is the gospel message, not simply the fact that Christ died for sin.

Historical Examples

Both Jesus' teaching and His experience indicate that some people respond with false, uncommitted faith and

23

others with true, submissive faith. The responses, though opposite, initially seem identical. But we learn that there is a qualitative difference between them, despite nonlordship teaching.

For instance, in the kingdom parables there are several illustrations of false professing, nonconverted people involved in the kingdom of heaven. Examples include the tares among the wheat (Matt. 13:24–30) and the bad fish among the good (Matt. 13:47–50). The Lord even tells us that these have responded to the same preached word—and some even appear initially to evidence the same salvation. In the parable of the sower the *same word* is received, but in different ways (Matt. 13:4–9). Only the fruitful reception is the true one; the other apparent receptions of the gospel are shown to be false (Matt. 13:18–33). In these examples the tares, bad fish, and unfruitful plants represent false professions of faith.

In John 2:23 we learn that many "believe" in Christ. But Jesus refuses to commit Himself to them—a remarkable response to new believers (John 2:24). By all external appearance these are true believers. But Jesus knows their hearts!

In the case of Judas, who undoubtedly was lost (John 6:70–71; Acts 1:25), the other disciples were confident of his "belief." For a time it appeared genuine: "Then Jesus said to *the twelve*, 'Do you also want to go away?' Then Simon Peter answered Him, 'Lord, to whom shall we go? You have the words of eternal life. Also *we* have come to believe and know that You are the Christ, the Son of the living God" (John 6:67–69). Despite Peter's confidence in the belief of "the twelve,"

24

Jesus knew their hearts: "Jesus answered them, 'Did I not choose you, the twelve, and one of you is a devil?' He spoke of Judas Iscariot, the son of Simon, for it was he who would betray Him, being one of the twelve" (John 6:70–71).

In John 8:30 we read, "As He spoke these words, many believed in Him." But as in John 2:23–24 and John 6:67–71, Christ's analysis exposes the true nature of their alleged faith:

> Then Jesus said *to those Jews who believed Him,* "If you abide in My word, you are My disciples indeed. And you shall know the truth, and the truth shall make you free." They answered Him, "We are Abraham's descendants, and have never been in bondage to anyone. How can you say, 'You will be made free'?" Jesus answered them, "Most assuredly, I say to you, whoever commits sin is a slave of sin. And a slave does not abide in the house forever, but a son abides forever. Therefore if the Son makes you free, you shall be free indeed. I know that you are Abraham's descendants, but you seek to kill Me, because *My word has no place in you.* . . . You do the deeds of your father." Then they said to Him, "We were not born of fornication; we have one Father, God." (John 8:31–37, 41)

Another illustration of false, empty faith is Simon Magus. He is said to have believed (Acts 8:13a) and on that basis was baptized (Acts 8:13b). But a short time later (Acts 8:14), Peter declared that he would "perish" because he was not truly among the redeemed and needed to repent: "But Peter said to him, 'Your money perish with you, because you thought that the gift of God could be purchased with money! You have neither part nor portion in this matter, for your heart is not right in the sight of God. Repent therefore of this your wickedness, and pray God if perhaps the thought of your heart may be forgiven you. For I see that you are poisoned by bitterness and bound by iniquity" (Acts 8:20–23).

John notes in his first epistle that even antichrists had been accepted among the believers: "Little children, it is the last hour; and as you have heard that the Antichrist is coming, even now many antichrists have come, by which we know that it is the last hour. They went out from us, but they were not of us; for if they had been of us, they would have continued with us; but they went out that they might be made manifest, that none of them were of us" (1 John 2:18–19). Notice he clearly states that had these antichrists truly been "of us," they would have "continued with us." They did not persevere in their professed faith in Christ. Hence, the danger of "false brethren" (2 Cor. 11:26; Gal. 2:4).

The Nature of Salvation

James strongly urges that faith will evidence itself in vitality and works (James 2:14–26). We are justified by faith; but that faith is never alone—it will express itself by its living nature. When James says that one is justified by works, he means that good works are the evidence that a person has saving faith. This evidential justification is sanctification in action. And it is vitally related to lordship salvation. For when one truly believes in Christ as Lord and Savior, then his new pattern of life will indicate that he has been regenerated. How would the nonsubmissive faith of Ryrie's "carnal Christian" measure up to James's questions in verse 14: "What does it profit, my brethren, if someone says he has faith but does not have works? Can [such] faith save him?"

Far too many people claim to believe in Christ as Savior, while living as if He never existed. This acceptance does as much for one's own soul as did Tetzel's indulgences in the sixteenth century. Empty faith, however popular today, is not saving faith.

Out of an inborn desire for self-preservation (Eccl. 3:11, NASB), people may accept the escape route of easy belief to avoid eternal hell. Not being under true conviction of the Holy Spirit, they do not want to be saved from sin and self in order to live holy lives for God. True faith is not a self-centered way of escape. It is a life principle (Heb. 11; James 2; Rom. 1:17) that in its binding nature directs one's confidence and trust into Christ the Lord.

The reason we may expect submission to the Lord and fruitful living among the truly redeemed is that God has wrought a fundamental change within them. True belief is not an unaided act or a mere addition to an unchanged life. Salvation involves a radical change within a person's life produced from above.

The Bible says the Christian is blessed "with every spiritual blessing" (Eph. 1:3). God's "divine power has given to us all things that pertain to life and godliness, through the knowledge of Him who called us by glory and virtue" (2 Peter 1:3).

We are under the power of grace, not sin: "Sin shall

not have dominion over you, for you are not under law but under grace" (Rom. 6:14).

The Holy Spirit and Christ indwell us: "But you are not in the flesh but in the Spirit, if indeed the Spirit of God dwells in you. Now if anyone does not have the Spirit of Christ, he is not His" (Rom. 8:9; cp. 1 Cor. 3:16; 6:19; 2 Cor. 6:16; Gal. 2:20).

Through the sovereign action of God, the Christian has been resurrected and made alive: "And you, being dead in your trespasses and the uncircumcision of your flesh, He has made alive together with Him, having forgiven you all trespasses" (Col. 2:13; cp. John 5:2, 24; Rom. 6:4–9). Thus, the Christian has a new life: "Most assuredly, I say to you, he who hears My word and believes in Him who sent Me has everlasting life, and shall not come into judgment, but has passed from death into life" (John 5:24; cp. John 3:36; 6:67; 1 John 5:11).

We have at all times Christ above us interceding for us: "Who is he who condemns? It is Christ who died, and furthermore is also risen, who is even at the right hand of God, who also makes intercession for us" (Rom. 8:34; cp. Heb. 7:25). This verse ties together His death and His intercession for us. Is His death effective? Why not His intercession? In fact, "We know that whoever is born of God does not sin; but he [Christ] who has been born of God keeps [him], and the wicked one does not touch him" (1 John 5:18). The sinning here is the present active indicative in Greek. It indicates habitual action. Because of Christ's work for and in us, we cannot live in habitual rebellion against God.

Faith and Salvation

The Christian has a new heart or character (Ezek. 36:26; cp. Ezek. 11:19) from the moment of regeneration. He, therefore, is a "new man" (Eph. 4:22–24; Col. 3:9–10) and a "new creation" (2 Cor. 5:17; Gal. 6:15; Eph. 2:10).

Conclusion

In summary, we have noted several facts concerning faith:

The Greek terms for "faith" are formed from the word root *pith*. The fundamental idea of this word base is "bind," which carries the obvious significance of submission. The Greek words for "faith" mean "to trust, to rely upon" and are occasionally used in parallel with "obey."

The case structures of Greek prepositions show that true faith is directed *into* the person of the Lord Jesus. True faith is not merely a belief of facts about Him. Because of this union sealed by faith, faith becomes a life principle that *will* evidence itself.

As quoted earlier, Gerstner writes in this regard: "The question is not whether good works are necessary to salvation, but in what way are they necessary. As the inevitable outworking of saving faith, they are necessary for salvation. As the meritorious ground of justification, they are not necessary *or acceptable*."[16] The champion of salvation by grace through faith, Martin Luther, taught that "works [are] the necessary result of the mercies of God bestowed in His gracious, immediate justification."[17]

Notes

1. Zane C. Hodges, *Absolutely Free! A Biblical Reply to Lordship Salvation* (Grand Rapids: Zondervan, 1989), 19.

2. Charles C. Ryrie, *Balancing the Christian Life* (Chicago: Moody, 1969), 179.

3. Hodges, *Absolutely Free!*, 38.

4. Ibid., 27.

5. Ryrie, *Balancing the Christian Life*, 35.

6. John R. W. Stott, *Basic Christianity* (Grand Rapids: Eerdmans, 1958), 114.

7. Bruce M. Metzger, *Lexical Aids for Students of New Testament Greek* (Princeton: the author, 1973), 48.

8. W. Baur, *A Greek-English Lexicon of the New Testament*, trans. and rev. W. F. Arndt and F. W. Gingrich (Chicago: University of Chicago, 1957), 668–70.

9. W. E. Vine, *An Expository Dictionary of New Testament Words* (Old Tappan, N.J.: Revell, 1941), 1:116.

10. Rudolf Bultmann, *"pisteuo," Theological Dictionary of the New Testament*, ed. Gerhard Kittel, trans. and ed. Geoffery W. Bromiley (Grand Rapids: Eerdmans, 1968), 6:175.

11. Ibid., 205.

12. John R. W. Stott, "Must Christ Be Lord to Be Savior— Yes!," *Eternity* 10 (Sept. 1959): 13ff.

13. James Hope Moulton, *A Grammar of New Testament Greek* (Edinburgh: T & T Clark, 1949), 1:67–68. My transliteration of the Greek.

14. A. T. Robertson, *A Grammar of the Greek New Testament in the Light of Historical Research* (Nashville: Broadman, 1934), 453.

15. James Hastings, ed., *The Christian Doctrine of Faith* (New York: Charles Scribner's Sons, 1919), 185.

16. John H. Gerstner, *Wrongly Dividing the Word of Truth:*

A Critique of Dispensationalism (Brentwood, Tenn.: Wolgemuth & Hyatt, 1991), 210, his emphasis.

17. J. D. Hannah, "The Meaning of Saving Faith: Luther's Interpretation of Romans 3:28," *Bibliotheca Sacra* 140 (Oct.–Dec. 1983): 328.

3

Repentance and Salvation

I kept back nothing that was helpful, but proclaimed it to you, and taught you publicly and from house to house, testifying to Jews, and also to Greeks, repentance toward God and faith toward our Lord Jesus Christ. (Acts 20:20–21)

A second major point of contention in the lordship controversy is the much abused doctrine of repentance. A proper understanding of the soteriological aspects of repentance is essential in any discussion of the means of salvation. Often the waters have been muddied by dispensational thinking on this issue. As mentioned earlier, not all dispensationalists are nonlordship; John MacArthur is a shining example of a dispensational lordship advocate. Yet dispensational theology is generally opposed to lordship salvation owing to a commitment to the concept of unconditional covenants. The supposedly unconditional covenant established with

Abraham guarantees the supremacy of ethnic Israel in a future millennium, argue dispensationalists. This unconditionality principle, as I noted in chapter 1, affects the dispensational understanding of committed faith in Christ.[1]

The Problem

In his *Systematic Theology*, Lewis Sperry Chafer spends several pages building a case against the inclusion of repentance in the gospel message. One avenue he explores is comparing how often "believe" or "faith" occurs with "repent" in the gospel of John and Romans. He finds that "repent" occurs only once in the two books combined. Chafer regards this argument from silence as "an overwhelming mass of irrefutable evidence" to the effect that "it is clear that the New Testament does not impose repentance upon the unsaved as a condition of salvation."[2] Those who preach repentance and faith, he contends, display an "all-but-universal disposition to confuse the vital issues."[3]

Hodges and Ryrie also make an issue of how many times the word "repent" occurs in John.[4] Hodges even holds that such an argument from silence "is the death knell for lordship theology." Repentance, he argues, is wholly optional.[5]

In dealing with the command to repent in Acts 2:38, Ryrie relegates repentance to a Jewish need to understand Christ's person differently. He says of this and all other calls for repentance:

34

The content of repentance which brings eternal life, and that which Peter preached on the day of Pentecost, is a change of mind about Jesus Christ. Whereas the people who heard Him on that day formerly thought of Him as mere man, they were asked to accept Him as Lord (Deity) and Christ (promised Messiah). To do this would bring salvation.[6]

Elsewhere he writes: "Is repentance a condition for receiving eternal life? Yes, if it is repentance or changing one's mind about Jesus Christ. No, if it means to be sorry for sin or even to resolve to turn from sin, for these things *will not save.*"[7] Indeed, repentance is "a false addition to faith," when proclaimed in evangelistic preaching.[8]

Thus, the nonlordship advocates see repentance from sin as absolutely unnecessary for receiving salvation in Christ. Repentance as "a change of mind" seems to be simply a bettering of one's Christological insight rather than a soteriological requirement. Ironically, given Ryrie's view of repentance as changing the mind about who Christ is, it would seem that John's gospel *should* have "repent" throughout it. Consider John's express purpose for writing his gospel: "But these are written, that you may believe that *Jesus is the Christ, the Son of God,* and that believing you may have life in His name" (John 20:31). Does this not involve Ryrie's view of repentance?

Advocates of the lordship doctrine of salvation speak clearly and pointedly of the virtue of divinely wrought repentance from sin. Louis Berkhof says that the repentance necessary for salvation is "a change of purpose, an inward turning away from sin, and a disposition to seek pardon and cleansing."[9] J. I. Packer ties the issue to the lordship controversy when he writes, "The repentance that Christ requires of His people consists in a settled refusal to set any limits to the claims which He may make on their lives."[10] He further adds that "where there is no clear knowledge, and hence no realistic recognition of the real claims that Christ makes, there can be no repentance, and therefore no salvation."[11]

These two theologians set forth a view clearly contradictory to the nonlordship position. As mentioned before, the repentance question is not always divided along eschatological lines, as may appear from the sources quoted. For example, E. Schuyler English, editor of *The New Scofield Reference Bible* and an ardent dispensationalist, agrees on the necessity of repentance, when he comments:

> There are some godly Bible students who oppose the teaching and preaching of repentance for this age. . . . They submit that salvation today is entirely by grace and that therefore the act of repentance on the part of the sinner suggests that there is something that he can do toward his salvation. But we believe this to be false reasoning. . . .[12]

Even some nonlordship advocates recognize the significance of preaching repentance. Warren W. Wiersbe, who wrote the foreword to Ryrie's *So Great Salvation*, says elsewhere:

> The biblical message is "repentance toward God, and faith toward our Lord Jesus Christ" (Acts 20:21), and

the two go together. Unless we turn from our sins, we cannot put saving faith in Jesus Christ. It is unfortunate that some preachers have so ignored the doctrine of repentance that their "converts" lack a true sense of conviction of sin. Balanced evangelism presents to the sinner both repentance and faith.[13]

Certainly there has been a wrong attitude about the nature of repentance in history. Simon Stylites, the fourth-century pole-sitter, and others have imported foreign ideas into the concept. The biblical demand for true, godly repentance from sin, however, should not be set aside for fear of such superstitious extremes. The remainder of this chapter will be given to defining and defending the biblical doctrine of repentance.

Biblical Terms for "Repentance"

In the Koine Greek of Scripture, two words are translated "repent." One is *metamelomai,* with its noun form *metameleia* (the noun does not occur in the New Testament). The other is *metanoeo,* with its noun form *metanoia.* *Metamelomai* only occurs six times in four passages of the New Testament, while *metanoeo* occurs thirty-four times and *metanoia* twenty-three times.

Sometimes confusion over repentance results from an improper distinction between these two words. The idea that repentance for sin is merely some sort of emotional show or other outward manifestation is erroneous. Examination of the original terminology helps to dispel this notion.

Metamelomai

Metamelomai is derived etymologically from a combination of the preposition *meta*, meaning "after," and the verb *melo*, which has the sense of "feeling, care, concern, or regret."[14] The word *metamelomai* carries the idea that is commonly confused with salvatory repentance, i.e. "to be emotionally sorrowful after an event." In the Septuagint (the Greek translation of the Hebrew Old Testament) the term signifies remorse as "a natural emotion following impudent and unjust action."[15] The idea of *natural remorse* stands preeminently in the meaning of the term.

In 2 Corinthians 7:8a Paul uses *metamelomai* in a closely related sense, i.e. "to regret": ". . . even if I made you sorry with my letter, I do not regret it [*metamelomai*], though I did regret it [*metamelomen* from *metamelomai*]. . . ." In verse 9 he rejoices that as a result of that unregretted letter, they "sorrowed to repentance" (*elupethete eis metanoian*). Here outward, emotional grief or sorrow lead to true repentance, but that grief was only the fertile ground from which repentance sprang—not the repentance itself. An outward show of sorrow may or may not indicate a genuine forsaking of sin.

Vincent well notes that *metamelomai* has "a meaning quite foreign to repentance in the ordinary gospel sense."[16] It is simply never used in the gospel message. No thought of the intellect or mind is contained in this word etymologically. It is primarily emotional sorrow, such as the repentance Judas felt as one who had wronged another (Matt. 27:3).

Metanoeo

Metanoeo comes from the conjoining of *meta* ("after") with *noeo* ("to perceive, think"), which is related to *nous* ("mind"). Thus it means "to perceive afterwards," implying a change of mind. Vine notes that in the New Testament it is always a change for the better.[17] This is the word employed in the gospel message.

Behm demonstrates that even in early Classical Greek usage, *metanoeo* had the sense of a change of mind that "derives from recognition that the earlier view was foolish, improper, or evil."[18] This recognition could affect the feelings, will, and intellect all at once and was "seldom a function of the intellect alone."[19] Nevertheless the mind, reason, attitude, or intellect stands out as preeminent, in contrast to the focus on emotion in the other term.

Repentance as a change of mind is clearly pictured in the parable of the prodigal son in Luke 15. The rebellious son views his degrading condition, and with his intellect he reasons, "I will arise and go to my father, and will say to him, 'Father, I have sinned against heaven and before you'" (Luke 15:18). He recognizes his utterly hopeless and sinful condition and decides to forsake this way of life to seek mercy from his father. He admits, "I . . . am no longer worthy to be called your son" (Luke 15:21). This is the "repentance [*metanoia*, noun form of *metanoeo*] toward God" which Paul preached (Acts 20:21), which Jesus meant when He said, "Unless you repent [*metanoeo*] you will all likewise perish" (Luke 13:3), and which the disciples were to preach "to all nations" (Luke 24:47).

The Nature of Repentance

Nonlordship Confusion

The biblical terminology makes it apparent that an emotional display is not a prerequisite to salvation. The lordship view certainly does not maintain that it is. The necessary ingredient in saving repentance is a true recognition of one's evil state and a decided, Spirit-prompted resolve to forsake sin and cast oneself on Christ's mercy. Great sorrow may well be involved, but it will grow out of an awareness of Christ's holiness seen against the background of one's own sinfulness.

Most biblical and linguistic scholars see no relationship between *metamelomai* and the gospel demand.[20] Chafer, however, in his word study of *metanoia* erroneously gives a "clear" example of non-saving repentance in an effort to show that the idea of repentance means simply a "change of mind" in general (i.e., about who Christ is and what He has done for the sinner). He lists Matthew 21:30, 32 as "a true example of the precise meaning of repentance" and concludes that repentance "is not an urge to self-condemnation" for sin.[21] In the midst of discussing passages where the word *metanoia* appears, Ryrie also cites Matthew 21:28–32, as if *metanoia* appears there. The Greek text of this passage employs *metamelomai* rather than *metanoia*, even though Ryrie claims that he is defining the term *metanoia*. Therefore, the passage has no real relation to the issue.

Whereas Chafer totally loses sight of repentance in the gospel, Ryrie radically changes its nature:

> The content of repentance which brings eternal life, and that which Peter preached on the day of Pentecost, is a change of mind about Jesus Christ. Whereas the people who heard him on that day formerly thought of Him as mere man, they were asked to accept Him as Lord (Deity) and Christ (Promised Messiah). To do this would bring salvation.[22]

This comment suggests that repentance had nothing whatsoever to do with sin and guilt, but that it simply was a change of mind as to the identity of Christ. It would seem that Ryrie has missed the thrust of Peter's message in Acts 2.

By declaring Christ to be more than a mere man, Peter emphasized the great and horrible sin of crucifying Him. Notice the emphasis: "Jesus of Nazareth, a Man attested by God . . . you have taken by *lawless* hands, have crucified, and put to death" (Acts 2:22, 23). And "God has made this Jesus, whom you [very emphatic use of the unnecessary personal pronoun] crucified, both Lord and Christ" (Acts 2:36). "Now when they heard this, they were cut to the heart" (Acts 2:37). The verb *katenugesan*, "cut" or "pricked" (KJV), means "'to be pierced, stabbed,' fig[urative] of the feeling of sharp pain connected w[ith] anxiety, remorse, etc. . . . Acts 2:37."[23]

Peter's listeners saw their sinfulness and were remorseful over it. That is when Peter preached, "Repent." The remorse was the fertile ground for their repentant resolve to turn from such an appalling, sinful way of life. Their change of mind about Christ made it necessary to forsake their sin and flee to Him.

41

Ryrie's view of repentance mysteriously overlooks this great barrier between God and man—sin!

Biblical Examples

Scriptural passages on the necessity of repentance are plentiful. Below are three clear examples.

First, in Matthew 12 the Lord compares His ministry with Jonah's at Ninevah. The result of Jonah's preaching was that the Ninevites repented in sackcloth (Jonah 3:8; Matt. 12:41). The sackcloth clearly pictured the mournful attitude of a person (2 Sam. 3:31); with the Ninevites it evidenced the sorrow for their sinfulness before God. They saw their sin and resolved to forsake it. Those to whom Jesus spoke were encouraged to do the same.

Second, in Luke 7:37–50 a sinful woman came weeping to Jesus. The Lord recognized her repentant attitude as faith (Luke 7:50) and forgave her sins. The weeping was certainly the result of her own knowledge of her sin and Christ's holiness. Her weeping was not necessary for salvation, but the repentance that prompted it was.

Third, in Matthew 19 the rich young ruler came to Christ sincerely believing that he himself had not sinned (Matt. 19:20). When Jesus pointed out his covetousness for riches and demanded that he forsake it, he went away sorrowful, not wishing to change his attitude. He was not told "simply believe," but "go, sell" (v. 21). His failure to repent of covetousness was an insurmountable barrier between him and salvation.

Biblical Demands

The necessity of repentance can be established from at least five avenues of proof.

First, it was preached by divinely ordained men before the resurrection of Christ: John the Baptist (Matt. 3:8; Luke 3:8; Acts 13:24), Jesus (Matt. 4:17; 11:20; Luke 13:3, 5), and the disciples (Mark 6:12).

Second, it was preached by divinely ordained men after the resurrection: Peter (Acts 2:38; 3:19; 5:31; 8:22; 11:18), and Paul (Acts 20:21; 26:20). The summary of the apostolic evangelistic message was that they were, in the words of Paul, "testifying to Jews, and also to the Greeks, repentance toward God and faith toward our Lord Jesus Christ" (Acts 20:21).

Third, God commands it (Acts 17:30; 26:30; Rom. 2:4; 2 Tim. 2:25). The universal call to repentance is clear: ". . . these times of ignorance God overlooked, but now commands all men everywhere to repent" (Acts 17:30).

Fourth, the Holy Spirit convicts of sin to prepare the heart for Christ: "And when He has come, He will convict the world of sin, and of righteousness, and of judgment" (John 16:8).

Fifth, repentance is vitally related to salvation: (1) Commands to repent may stand alone, without reference to faith (Luke 13:3; 15:7; 24:17; Acts 17:30). (2) The command to repent is sometimes found along with references to faith (Matt. 21:32; Mark 1:15; Acts 19:4; 20:21; Heb. 6:1). When it is, repentance is always mentioned first. (3) Repentance can by synonymous with faith (Rom. 2:4; 2 Tim. 2:25). (4) Those who repent are considered believers (Acts 2:38–47; 3:19; 11:17–18).

Repentance as a means of salvation is, like faith, impossible to the natural man (Jer. 13:23; Prov. 27:22; Matt. 19:21–26). People love sin and do not wish to forsake it (John 3:16–19). When they do respond to the demand to repent, it is because of God's sovereign initiative. Repentance, or the enablement to repent, is a gift of God (Acts 5:31; 11:18; Rom. 2:4; 2 Tim. 2:25). "When they heard these things, they became silent; and they glorified God, saying, 'Then God has also granted to the Gentiles repentance to life'" (Acts 11:18).

Repentance and John's Gospel

Even though, as Chafer, Hodges, and Ryrie note, one cannot find the term *metanoia* in John, this in no way weakens the demand for calling men to repentance for salvation. There are several problems with this argument from silence concerning *metanoia*.

In the first place, the reality may exist apart from the verbal token. The doctrine of the Trinity is nowhere explicitly stated in Scripture. It is, however, intricately woven into the very fabric of the Bible even though the word does not occur. Likewise, if Christ speaks against sin in John while calling His listeners to faith, then the absence of the word "repent" carries little weight. And Christ certainly does speak against sin.

After Christ healed the crippled man, He commanded the man: "See, you have been made well. Sin no more, lest a worse thing come upon you" (John 5:14). Surely the Lord had in mind the man's need of salvation when He urged Him to avoid sin.

In His evangelistic encounter with the Samaritan woman, Jesus pointed out her sinfulness: "The woman said to Him, 'Sir, give me this water, that I may not thirst, nor come here to draw.' Jesus said to her, 'Go, call your husband, and come here.' The woman answered and said, 'I have no husband.' Jesus said to her, 'You have well said, "I have no husband," for you have had five husbands, and the one whom you now have is not your husband; in that you spoke truly'" (John 4:15–18). Jesus' reference to her husband was obviously intended to point out her moral failure in this area of her life.

When Jesus dealt with the woman caught in adultery, His parting words of forgiveness included an exhortation to "go and sin no more" (John 8:11). When many allegedly believed in Him (John 8:30–31; cp. 37, 41, 44), He confronted them on the sin question: "Most assuredly, I say to you, whoever commits sin is a servant of sin. And a slave does not abide in the house forever, but a son abides forever. Therefore if the Son makes you free, you shall be free indeed" (John 8:34–36). The saving freedom He offered was freedom from sin's dominion.

Second, we must recognize the preeminent purpose of John's gospel. He tells us very plainly that He was writing it so that the readers would know who Christ is and that they might believe. So it is quite natural that faith is emphasized: "And truly Jesus did many other signs in the presence of His disciples, which are not written in this book; but these are written that you may believe that Jesus is the Christ, the Son of God, and that believing you may have life in His name" (John 20:30–31).

Third, the evangelical urging of repentance is found elsewhere in the New Testament message. As I have shown, references to repentance are common in the New Testament, occurring over sixty times. We should use the fullest revelation of God to establish our doctrine, not simply a portion of it—nor especially a partial understanding of that one portion.

Conclusion

The lordship view of salvation adequately deals with man's need for salvation in terms of his actual transgression. The gift of salvation is not an indulgence for sin, but rather a remedy for it. The gospel message, to be sure, is not *faith plus works*. But it is *faith that works*—in and with repentance. As John Murray observes of the faith-repentance relationship: "There is no priority. The faith that is unto salvation is a penitent faith and the repentance that is unto life is a believing repentance."[24]

The previous chapter demonstrated the character of faith that is necessary for salvation—an obedient, humble believing "into" the person of Christ. The need for faith among the Jews (as among all men) is a "need to turn from falsehood to truth. They need to set aside all their previous standards and judgments. This renunciation of the world, this turning of man from himself, is the primary meaning of faith. It is man's self-surrender, his turning to the invisible ([John] 20:29) and sovereign."[25]

Such a faith as required by Christ is a forsaking faith, thus, a repentant faith. It is impossible to separate true faith from true repentance. Both are present in the response of the soul to the effectual calling of God. To turn to God is to turn from sin. The negative aspect of conversion is repentance, or turning from sin; the positive aspect is a reaching out to Christ in self–abnegating faith.

A person cannot truly trust and receive Christ as Savior while consciously clinging to sin, which militates against Christ's nature. Certainly more sin will be discovered in one's life as he spiritually matures, but deliberately stowing away sin is an act of defiance and cannot coexist with saving faith. Christ, the Lord of glory (1 Cor. 2:8), detests sin and will have no one come to Him while remaining in love with his sin. In fact, love of sin is the very thing that keeps people from coming to Christ (John 3:19).

Notes

1. See O. T. Allis, *Prophecy and the Church* (Philadelphia: Presbyterian and Reformed, 1945), 43.

2. Lewis Sperry Chafer, *Systematic Theology* (Dallas: Dallas Seminary, 1948), 3:376.

3. Ibid., 371.

4. Zane C. Hodges, *Absolutely Free! A Biblical Reply to Lordship Salvation* (Grand Rapids: Zondervan, 1989), 148; cp. 26, 146–48. Charles C. Ryrie, *So Great Salvation* (Wheaton, Ill.: Victor, 1989), 97.

5. Hodges, *Absolutely Free!*, 158.

6. Charles C. Ryrie, *Balancing the Christian Life* (Chicago: Moody, 1969), 176.

7. Ryrie, *So Great Salvation*, 99.

8. *The Ryrie Study Bible* (Chicago: Moody, 1976), 1950.

9. Louis Berkhof, *Systematic Theology* (Grand Rapids: Eerdmans, 1941), 486.

10. J. I. Packer, *Evangelism and the Sovereignty of God* (Downer's Grove, Ill.: InterVarsity, 1961), 72.

11. Ibid., 73.

12. E. Schuyler English, *Things Surely to Be Believed* (Neptune, N.J.: Loizeaux, 1956), 1:189.

13. Warren W. Wiersbe, *The Bible Exposition Commentary* (Wheaton, Ill.: Victor, 1989), 1:414.

14. Bryon H. Dement, "Repentance," *The International Standard Bible Encyclopedia*, ed. James Orr (Grand Rapids: Eerdmans, 1965), 4:2558.

15. O. Michel, *"metanoia,"* *Theological Dictionary of the New Testament*, ed. Gerhard Kittel, trans. and ed. Geoffery W. Bromiley (Grand Rapids: Eerdmans, 1968), 4:626.

16. Marvin R. Vincent, *Word Studies in the New Testament* (Grand Rapids: Eerdmans, 1965), 1:116.

17. W. E. Vine, *An Expository Dictionary of New Testament Words* (Old Tappan, N.J.: Revell, 1941), 279.

18. Johannes Behm, *"metanoeo,"* *Theological Dictionary of the New Testament*, 4:977.

19. Ibid., p. 978.

20. For example: Robert L. Dabney, *Lectures in Systematic Theology* (Grand Rapids: Eerdmans, 1972), 351ff.; Alfred Edersheim, *The Life and Times of Jesus the Messiah* (Grand Rapids: Eerdmans, 1965), 2:421; William Hendriksen, *The Gospel According to Matthew* (Grand Rapids: Baker, 1973), 779. Richard C. Trench, *Synonyms of the New Testament* (Grand Rapids: Eerdmans, 1969), 256. Vincent, *Word Studies*, 1:116.

21. Chafer, *Systematic Theology*, 3:372.

22. Ryrie, *Balancing the Christian Life*, 176.

23. W. Baur, *A Greek-English Lexicon of the New Testament*,

trans. and rev. W. F. Arndt and F. W. Gingrich (Chicago: University of Chicago, 1957), 416.

24. John Murray, *Redemption: Accomplished and Applied* (Grand Rapids: Eerdmans, 1955), 113.

25. Rudolf Bultmann, *"pisteuo,"* *Theological Dictionary of the New Testament*, 6:223.

4

The Lordship of Christ and Salvation

If you confess with your mouth the Lord Jesus and believe in your heart that God has raised Him from the dead, you will be saved. For with the heart one believes to righteousness, and with the mouth confession is made to salvation. (Rom. 10:9–10)

In this chapter we will consider the lordship question within a narrower scope. The two sides to the debate are again at opposite poles when it comes to interpreting Jesus' title "Lord." Neither evangelical camp denies that Christ is an eternal member of the Trinity and thus fully God. That is not the issue here. The question simply stated is, What does the title "Lord" signify, and how does it affect the presentation of Christ as Savior?

51

The Problem

In the apostolic church, Jesus Christ was preached as the only hope for sinful man. It is interesting to note that He is referred to as "Savior" twice in the book of Acts, while He is referred to as "Lord" ninety-two times. This designation of Christ as Lord must have some soteriological significance because of its frequent mention in the apostles' evangelistic preaching. In the epistles, as well, He is called "Lord" hundreds of times.

Ryrie renders the various uses of the term "lord" (*kurios*) in the New Testament as: God (Acts 3:22), owner (Luke 19:33), sir (John 4:11), idols (1 Cor. 8:5), and one's husband (1 Peter 3:6). He then suggests that, when used of Christ, "Lord" could be simply a title of respect. He adds, however, that "it must also have had some unusual connotation which caused some to question its validity. . . . In other words, when someone who apparently was not more than an ordinary man . . . claimed to be God, and when the title Lord . . . became attached to this Man Jesus in the preaching of the apostles, then there was division. . . . if it meant 'God Jesus' or 'Jehovah Jesus,' then one can account for the division and debate over that kind of claim."[1] Thus, Ryrie's contention is that *kurios* primarily means "God" when used of Christ. This would be the general consensus among non-lordship proponents.

The lordship view of the ascription of the title "Lord" to Christ agrees that it involves Christ's deity. But it is more than a term of identity—it is also a term of *relationship*. Granted, *kurios* represents Christ as God, but would not also *theos* have been an adequate and interchangeable term—and possibly clearer? If Jesus Christ is presented as *kurios* in reference to His deity, then this term must highlight a particular aspect of His deity, that is, His sovereignty, majesty, rulership. That can be demonstrated by a review of the historical and etymological implications of the term.

One example of an extreme nonlordship presentation is this illustration from the pen of R. B. Thieme:

> It is possible, even *probable*, that when a believer out of fellowship falls for certain types of philosophy, if he is a logical thinker, he will become an "unbelieving believer." Yet believers who become agnostics are still saved; they are still born again. You can even become an *atheist*; but if you once accepted Christ as Savior, you cannot lose your salvation, even though you deny God.[2]

A similar statement is found in Ryrie's writing: "Normally one who has believed can be described as a believer; that is, one who continues to believe. But . . . a believer may come to a place of not believing, and yet God will not disown him, since He cannot disown Himself."[3]

These statements collide headlong with the biblical doctrines of perseverance and sanctification as they relate to the security of the true believer. All of these matters are vitally related to lordship and the very meaning of salvation.

Implications of the Term *Kurios*

Christ is so frequently called *kurios* in the New Testament—747 times—that there must be some special significance behind this term. Ryrie's position that it indicates only His deity is woefully deficient. The Scriptures employ many names to describe the infinitely perfect, multifaceted God of the universe. In the Old Testament He is called *Elohim, El Shaddai, Adonai,* and *Jehovah,* just for a few examples. In the New Testament He is known as "God," "Father," "Lord," "God of glory," "the living God," "the Most High," "the true God," etc. All of these names have special signification. The term "Lord" (*kurios*) especially has an enlightening lexical history.

Pre-New Testament Usage

In the Septuagint (the ancient Greek translation of the Hebrew Old Testament) *kurios* is used thousands of times to translate various Hebrew words. According to the Brown-Driver-Briggs *Lexicon,* God's revered covenant name *yhwh* ("Jehovah") occurs 6832 times.[4] Of these occurrences it is translated in the Septuagint by *kurios* 6156 times.[5] The term *adon* ("master") is used in reference to God thousands of times and is always translated by *kurios.* It is also used of men as a "respectful term of address," and in this usage is translated by *kurios* 192 times.[6] *Baal* ("owner") is translated by *kurios* fifteen times.[7] Other uses of *kurios* are: a slave's owner (Gen. 24:12), a woman's husband (Gen. 18:12), a court term (1 Sam. 26:17), a term of high veneration (Num.

11:28), and a term of politeness (Gen. 23:6). These are all translated from the Hebrew *adon*.

Though *adon* is so frequently used of God, Unger notes that it is "an early word denoting ownership, hence, absolute control. It is not properly a divine title, being used of the owner of slaves."[8] Brown-Driver-Briggs show the root idea of the word as originally being "firm, strong." It later took on the nuance of "determine, command, rule" and, thus, "put under command, rule over."[9]

Consequently, the historical significance of *adon* is not that it was initially a divine appellation. It *became* a divine title because of its emphasis on rulership, which would most perfectly fit God's absolute authority. The Septuagint translators obviously felt *kurios* was the ideal equivalent of *adon* because of its idea of "lordship."

Even more important to the understanding of the Septuagint usage of *kurios* is the exclusively divine name *yhwh* (Jehovah). It is quite consistently translated by *kurios*, indeed, 90 percent of the time. Concerning God's most common, covenant name, Brown-Driver-Briggs notes that "most [scholars] take it as Qal of *hwh* . . . , '*the one who is: i.e., the absolute and unchangeable one*' . . . '*the existing, everliving.*'"[10]

The significance of the Septuagint equation of *kurios* with *yhwh* is well expressed in the *Theological Dictionary of the New Testament*:

> Our present task is to discuss the reasons for the choice of the word *kurios* in the LXX [Septuagint]. . . . It is better to start with the Greek meaning of the word in the time of the LXX. . . . *Kurios* was not then used as an epithet for God in paganism. . . . At the time when

the specifically Hellenistic usage was first emerging, *kurios* denoted the one who has lawful power of disposal. . . .

The LXX makes strong and conscious affirmation of the fact that Yahweh's position as Lord is legitimate. This affirmation can be based on the historical fact of the election of Israel. He who redeemed Israel from the "iron furnace" of Egypt had thereby a right to this people. . . . The one word *kurios*. . . was of itself adequate to name a God, the one God. This must have suggested continually to its hearers God's unlimited control over all things.[11]

This idea is based on the historical derivation of the adjective *kurios* and the noun *kuros*. Both can be traced to the very early Indo–Germanic *keu* or *ku*, with the sense of "to swell," and ultimately "to be strong." In Classical Greek *kurios* was used of a military capture to denote possession; thus, "to be a *kurios* is to exert a powerful influence."[12]

In Classical Greek the word was rare and denoted the narrow sense of lord as an owner, i.e., the one with full authority. The obvious significance of gods' later being called *kurios* was a development from this idea of powerful authority.[13] Foerester emphatically notes that, except for *kurios* with the genitive, *kurios* was never used of gods or rulers prior to the first century B.C.[14] The idea of deity is historically and etymologically foreign to the term itself. Indeed, the term later expressed deity only because of what it implied in itself: rulership, authority. Interestingly, the Augustan and Hadrian imperial cults in the first two centuries employed *kurios*, but it had "nothing whatever to do with the divine predicate."[15]

New Testament Usage

The history of the Greek language dates back to 900 B.C. and continues to this day. The uninterrupted usage and development of Greek provides a wealth of material to illumine every word found in the New Testament. Historical linguistics and extrabiblical literature are vital tools in aiding one's study of the language of the New Testament. The New Testament writers did not create a new language, but wrote in a widely understood, highly expressive, vernacular—Koine Greek, the street language of the common man.

The earlier development of the word *kurios* ("lord, master") bore heavily upon the biblical usage of the term. *Kurios* was used frequently for "owner," for example, an owner of a vineyard (Matt. 20:8), a colt (Luke 19:33), a dog (Matt. 15:27), a steward (Luke 16:3), and a slave (Acts 16:16, 19). The term suggests an authoritative relationship between persons, or between persons and property. Foerester notes that "the superiority to which there must be submission is implied in *kurios* [in] 1 Pet. 3:6. . . ."[16] Sara, as Abraham's wife, was to be obediently submissive to him: thus, she called him "lord" (*kurios*).

This relationship is further illustrated in the usage of the term in such authoritative relationships as a slave to his owner (Matt. 13:27; 25:20); a worker to his employer (Luke 12:8); a citizen to the civil magistrate (Matt. 27:62–63); and a son to his father (Matt. 21:29). Each of these expresses the idea of submission and obedience to the person designated as *kurios*. In Colossians 3:22 the term "lord," as used in the reference of a slave to his owner, is defined by Paul. "Servants, obey in all things your masters according to the flesh, not with eye-service, as men-pleasers; but in sincerity of heart, fearing God." Foerester notes of this verse: "The reference is to a total obedience to the master which avoids [*opthalmodoulia*, "eye-service"], a mere show of service, and is thus whole-heartedly loyal."[17]

The verbal form of *kurios* is *kurieo*, which carries the force of "to be lord or master, rule, lord it (over), control."[18] The dominion or rule denoted in this verb is used in various ways in the New Testament. All of them exemplify the historical signification of the term: a king ruling with authority (Luke 22:25); the control of sin over the unregenerate (Rom. 6:9); the unbreakable power and dominion of death over sinners (Rom. 6:9). Paul uses it negatively to say that he himself cannot control a man's faith (2 Cor. 1:24). He also uses it in a positive sense when he speaks of Christ's having absolute dominion over the living and the dead (Rom. 14:9) and over earthly masters (1 Tim. 6:15). The intensified form of the term is *katakurieo*, which also occurs in the same sense (of dominion or authority) in Mark 10:42; Acts 19:16; and 1 Peter 5:2.

The linguistic evidence points quite strongly to the conclusion that *kurios* emphasizes controlling authority. When used of Christ in the frequent gospel preaching of Acts and the Epistles, it most certainly has to do with the acceptance of Jesus Christ as Lord in order to be Savior. Robinson well summarizes the reason for the common choice of this term to designate Christ: "God is the term of pure exaltation, while Lord carries with it more expressly the idea of sovereign rulership in actual practice, evoking obedient service."[19]

The preceding study in no way depreciates the doctrine of the deity of Christ. In fact, it adds much to the doctrine. Christ's deity can be clearly seen in such passages as John 1:1; 20:28; Philippians 2:6–8; Hebrews 1:8; 1 John 5:20; and many others. Christ is, at times, referred to as "our God and Savior," as in 2 Peter 1:1 and Titus 2:13. The grammatical construction employed in the last two verses is called the Granville Sharp Rule of the Article. It declares that Jesus is both God and Savior. His sovereign lordship flows naturally from His intrinsic being as it comes to bear on His saving work.

Jesus as *Kurios*

The evidence that *kurios* historically denotes rulership is overwhelming. As a divine appellation *kurios* is properly understood to ascribe this supreme rulership. Therefore, when either God the Father or God the Son is called *kurios*, it must be in recognition of the fact of sovereign ruler. Below are several Scripture passages that demonstrate this fact. I shall comment briefly on those verses, which are most relevant and which, ironically, Ryrie uses in an attempt to undermine the lordship position.

Romans 10:9

Romans 10:9 is probably one of the most common focal points in the lordship issue. As translated in the New American Standard Bible, the verse reads: "That if

you confess with your mouth Jesus as Lord, and believe in your heart that God raised Him from the dead,
you shall be saved." The American Standard Version
(1901) also has "Jesus as Lord," while the New English
Bible, Revised Standard Version, Today's English Version, New International Version and Williams translation have "Jesus is Lord."

Ryrie follows the King James Version, which renders the vital phrase, "confess with thy mouth the Lord
Jesus." He then insists that one must confess "Jesus as
God . . . the God-man,"[20] which, of course, is true. It is
not, however, the point of this passage. Again, it can be
assumed that *kurios* means God in the sense of the sovereign ruler. The lordship view sees in this phrase a
recognition or an "exact agreeing" (*homologeo*, "confess")
that Jesus is one's Lord or Master.

The grammatical construction places further emphasis on Christ's lordship. The absence of the Greek definite article before a word is exegetically significant. Dana
and Mantey note concerning the absence of the article
before a noun, "This places stress upon the *qualitative*
aspect of the noun rather than its mere identification."[21]
This verse, then, should be understood as saying that
Jesus is Lord qualitatively, that is, in dominion, authority, rule. The unsaved man will not confess Jesus as
Master. And this is the vital difference between the saved
and the lost: one is ruled by Christ, while the other is
under the *kurieo* ("dominion") of sin (Rom. 6:9).

Acts 2:36

In the New American Standard Bible, Acts 2:36
reads: "Therefore let all the house of Israel know for

certain that God has made Him both Lord and Christ—
this Jesus whom you crucified."

Ryrie uses this passage to buttress his interpretation
of Romans 10:9, that "Jesus the Man had been proved
by the resurrection and ascension to be Lord, God and
Christ the Messiah."[22] Ryrie's claim is deficient for several reasons.

First, Ryrie is admittedly referring to Romans 1:4,
where the resurrection "declared Him to be the Son of
God with power." The phrase "Son of God" obviously
refers to Jesus' deity. Romans 1:4, however, says He
was "declared" to be so—not "made," as in Acts 2:36.
The two verses express different truths and must be
properly distinguished. "Declare" is a proper translation of the aorist participle *horisthentos*, which is derived from *horizo*, to "appoint, designate, declare."[23] God
declared that Jesus was His divine Son through the
resurrection.

Second, in the Greek of Acts 2:36 the verb "has
made" is the aorist form of *poieo*. This very reference is
cited in the major lexicon of our day as meaning "*to make
someone* or someth[ing] (into) someth[ing]."[24] This verb,
poieo, never means "to declare." It always has reference
to "doing, making, creating," etc. The verse says that
God made Christ to be Lord. Certainly God the Father
did not make Christ to be God—He has always been
God, even during His time of humiliation on earth.

Third, Peter in the context shows that Christ as the
crucified man was resurrected and ascended into glory.
He repeatedly speaks of Christ's present position: He
was raised to sit on His throne (Acts 2:30); He is highly
exalted (2:33); He is sitting at God's right hand until His

foes are made a footstool (2:34–34). So, Acts 2:36 speaks of God's "making" Christ the sovereign ruler of the earth. This is the reason all judgment is committed to Christ (John 5:22, 27). He became man, lived as man, died as man, and now is exalted as man to be Lord and to judge men.

This same idea is expressed in Philippians 2:8–11, where His exaltation "is above every name, that at the name of Jesus every knee should bow . . . and that every tongue should confess that Jesus Christ is Lord." Christ was "humble" and "obedient" unto death; now God has made Him the Lord of life before whom all others must bow.

1 Corinthians 12:3

In 1 Corinthians 12:3 Paul writes, "Therefore I make known to you, that no one speaking by the Spirit of God says, 'Jesus is accursed'; and no one can say, 'Jesus is Lord,' except by the Holy Spirit" (NASB). As expected, Ryrie interprets this verse to mean that no one can call Jesus "God" except under the influence of the Holy Spirit. That interpretation may be permissible, but Ryrie misrepresents the lordship view when he writes, "Lord in this sense must mean Jehovah-God for the simple reason that unsaved people can and do say Lord, meaning Sir, in reference to Christ."[25] The lordship view to which Ryrie is supposedly addressing himself would not translate the idiom to mean "Sir," but rather "Lord, Master."

There are at least two problems with Ryrie's interpretation. First, the Greek construction here is the same as that in Romans 10:9. There is no definite article before "Lord." The Greek is simply *kurios Hiesous*. Thus, the statement is qualitative: Jesus is Lord or Master to the one under the impulse of the Holy Spirit, that is, to the believer. An unbeliever does not want Christ to be his Master.

Second, the contrast of "accursed" with "Lord" is significant. If one looks upon Jesus as an accursed person, that is the opposite of deeming Him as Master. The passage has two types of people in view. One wants nothing to do with Christ and even calls Him "accursed." The other loves Christ and deems Him Master. The believer stands in stark contrast to the unbelieving idol-worshiper.

Other Passages

Below, very briefly, are a few of many other evidences that Jesus must be acknowledged as Lord and Master.

First, when Thomas saw the risen Christ, he cried out: "My Lord and my God!" (John 20:28). Surely he was not saying, "My God and my God." He recognized Him as Master and God.

Second, the members of the apostolic church employed "Lord" in their references to Christ when they told others about Him. They seemed to make a conscious effort to preach Him as the Master to whom all must commit themselves. "And it shall come to pass that whoever calls on the name of the Lord shall be saved" (Acts 2:21). "The word which God sent to the children of Israel, preaching peace through Jesus

Christ—He is Lord of all" (Acts 10:36). He is called "Lord" 146 times in Acts through Revelation.

Third, the apostolic church emphasized His supreme exalted rule. The sovereign ruler does not seek half-hearted profession. "Him God has exalted to His right hand to be Prince and Savior, to give repentance to Israel and forgiveness of sins. And we are His witnesses of these things and so also is the Holy Spirit whom God has given to those who *obey* him" (Acts 5:31–32). "Therefore God also has highly exalted Him and given Him the name which is above every name, that at the name of Jesus every knee should *bow*" (Phil. 2:9–10a; cp. Rom. 14:7–8, 11). When He comes it will be "in flaming fire taking vengeance on those who do not know God, and on those who *do not obey* the gospel of our *Lord* Jesus Christ" (2 Thess. 1:8). Lordship involves obedience.

Fourth, the apostolic church expressly described its preaching as an affirmation of Christ's lordship. "We do not preach ourselves but Christ Jesus as Lord, and ourselves as your bond-servants for Jesus' sake" (2 Cor. 4:5, NASB). "Some of them were men from Cyprus and Cyrene, who, when they had come to Antioch, spoke to the Hellenists, preaching the Lord Jesus" (Acts 11:20). ". . . preaching the kingdom of God and teaching the things which concern the Lord Jesus Christ with all confidence, no one forbidding him" (Acts 28:31).

Conclusion

The proper presentation of Christ as Savior involves His proclamation as Lord and Savior. Overwhelmingly the New Testament emphasizes His lordship, as was seen from three lines of evidence.

First, the term kurios, which is used hundreds of times of Christ, historically and etymologically denotes sovereign rulership.

Second, the term *kurios*, when used of God, demonstrates His sovereignty and rulership in the Old and New Testaments.

Third, explicit Scripture references associate Christ's lordship with salvation.

When Christ is truly believed "upon" or believed "into," He Himself is accepted for salvation. Thus Christ, being the Lord, comes into the heart of the believer as Lord and Master. To omit Christ's office of Lord in evangelistic preaching is to divide Christ and splinter the gospel message.

Notes

1. Charles C. Ryrie, *Balancing the Christian Life* (Chicago: Moody, 1969), 173.

2. R. B. Thieme, *Apes and Peacocks, of the Pursuit of Happiness* (Houston: the author, 1973), 23. Emphasis mine.

3. Charles C. Ryrie, *So Great Salvation* (Wheaton, Ill: Victor, 1989), 141.

4. F. Brown, S. R. Driver, and Charles A. Briggs, *A Hebrew and English Lexicon of the Old Testament* (London: Oxford, 1972), 217.

5. Gottried Quell, *"kurios," Theological Dictionary of the New Testament*, ed. Gerhard Kittel, trans. and ed. Geoffrey W. Bromiley (Grand Rapids: Eerdmans, 1965), 3:1058.

6. Ibid.

7. Ibid.

8. Merrill F. Unger, *Unger's Bible Dictionary* (Chicago: Moody, 1966), 665.

9. Brown, Driver, and Briggs, *Hebrew and English Lexicon*, 10.

10. Ibid., 218.

11. Werner Foerester, *"kurios,"* *Theological Dictionary of the New Testament*, 3:1081–82.

12. Johannes Behm, *"kurios,"* *Theological Dictionary of the New Testament*, 3:1041.

13. Foerester, *"kurios,"* 1046.

14. Ibid., 1049.

15. Ibid., 1056.

16. Ibid., 1086.

17. Ibid., 1095.

18. W. Baur, *A Greek-English Lexicon of the New Testament*, trans. and rev. W. F. Arndt and F. W. Gingrich (Chicago: University of Chicago, 1957), 459.

19. William Childs Robinson, "Lord," *Baker's Dictionary of Theology*, ed. Everett F. Harrison (Grand Rapids: Baker, 1960), 329.

20. Charles C. Ryrie, *Balancing the Christian Life* (Chicago: Moody, 1969), 175.

21. H. E. Dana and Julius R. Mantey, *A Manual Grammar of the Greek New Testament* (Toronto: Macmillan, 1955), 149.

22. Ryrie, *Balancing the Christian Life*, 175.

23. Baur, *Greek-English Lexicon*, 584.

24. Ibid., 688.

25. Ryrie, *Balancing the Christian Life*, 174.

5

Discipleship and Salvation

Then Jesus said to His disciples, "If anyone desires to come after Me, let him deny himself, and take up his cross, and follow Me. For whoever desires to save his life will lose it, and whoever loses his life for My sake will find it." (Matt. 16:24–25)

In this chapter all the other aspects reviewed become practical and vital, for herein is the heart of the gospel message, which Christ sent His disciples into the world to preach.

The Problem

In no other section of our study is the dividing line between the two camps so clearly drawn. Confusion reigns supreme on the discipleship question in the church today. The following quotations demonstrate the polarity of opinion over the issue.

Excerpts from three popular nonlordship publications illustrate their general attitudes regarding discipleship. In the foreword to Hodges's *The Hungry Inherit*, Ryrie writes: "The burden of this work is to *distinguish* clearly salvation and discipleship. *No distinction is more vital* to theology, [or] more basic to a correct understanding of the New Testament."[1]

Pentecost agrees with the distinction wholeheartedly: "Discipleship is frequently equated with salvation and erroneously made a condition for becoming a Christian."[2] He then fixes a great gulf between the believer and the disciple (super-believer), when he comments, "There is a *vast difference* between being saved and being a disciple."[3]

Hodges comments on John 6:67, "Here there is no confusion between discipleship and salvation, as there is today in lordship theology."[4]

Standing diametrically opposed to these views, lordship advocate John R. W. Stott writes: "Jesus never concealed the fact that in His religion there was a demand as well as an offer. Indeed, the demand was as total as the offer was free. . . . Jesus gave no encouragement whatever to thoughtless applicants for discipleship. . . . He sent irresponsible enthusiasts empty away."[5]

MacArthur expresses the lordship view thus: "The word *disciple* is used consistently as a synonym for *believer* throughout the book of Acts (6:1, 2, 7; 11:26; 14:20, 22; 15:10). Any distinction between the two words is purely artificial. . . . The call to Christian discipleship explicitly demands . . . total dedication. It is full commitment, with nothing knowingly or deliberately held back. No one can come to Christ on any other terms."[6]

Can any two opinions be more directly opposed? Although this book focuses on the initial problem in becoming a Christian (i.e., the proper presentation and acceptance of Christ), the discipleship question immediately blends into the doctrine of sanctification. The beginning of discipleship is the beginning of salvation, according to the lordship view. Therefore, it is extremely important to the debate.

Association of Pertinent Terms

The terminology involved in the discipleship passages is very clear. There is no linguistic warrant for dividing believers into two groups, believers and super-believers.

In each of its 269 occurrences in the King James Version the English noun "disciple" is translated from the Greek noun *mathetes*. The verb *matheteuo* occurs only four times and is rendered "instruct," "teach," and "disciple." The noun *mathetes* means "a pupil, apprentice, adherent."[7] It is often used to designate the followers of John the Baptist (e.g., Matt. 9:14; Luke 5:33), the Pharisees (e.g., Matt. 22:16; Mark 2:18), as well as those of Christ.

Thus *mathetes* ("disciple") is a common term involving little difficulty. The word does not distinguish between types of true believers for any reason, spiritual or otherwise. Even Pentecost and Zuck admit that it can refer to either curious spectators or believers in general.[8] The Baur-Arndt-Gingrich *Lexicon* notes that

Acts "uses *m[athetes]* almost exclusively to denote the members of the new religious community . . . so that it almost [equals] Christian."[9] As noted above, there are a number of passages in Acts that exemplify this truth. For instance, Acts 11:26 teaches that "disciples [believers] were first called Christians at Antioch." Those who distinguish believers into two groups must arbitrarily decide when *mathetes* is used of the average believer and when it is used of the super-believer.

The following summary of passages associated with discipleship indicates that Scripture does not distinguish between two classes of believers.

The Great Commission and Discipleship

The Lord's command to evangelize the world, commonly called the Great Commission, is given in Mark 16:15 and Matthew 28:19–20. The commission recorded in Luke 24:47 was probably given on a different occasion and therefore is not parallel with the other two.[10] Mark 16:15 offers the bare outline of the commission: "Go into all the world and preach the gospel to every creature." Matthew 28:19–20 presents a fuller statement: "Go therefore and make disciples of all nations, baptizing them in the name of the Father and of the Son and of the Holy Spirit, teaching them to observe all things that I have commanded you; and lo, I am with you always, even to the end of the age."[11]

The significance of these passages is obvious. The preaching of the gospel summarized in Mark is the making of disciples in Matthew. Even the ardent foe of lordship salvation Everett Harrison admits this "complication of terms" where "disciple is equivalent to convert or Christian."[12]

There is no "complication of terms" if one does not insist on making false distinctions. The lordship view sees discipleship as equivalent to entering into the new life of faith in Christ. The life of the disciple is the life of the true child of God.

Jesus on Discipleship

Despite much evidence to the contrary, nonlordship spokesmen make gradations among believers when they approach Jesus' discipleship passages. The following is a brief overview of several parables and discourses. All of these were given, according to the nonlordship view, concerning discipleship as a beyond-believing commitment.

The Two Builders

The parable of the two builders in Matthew 7 and Luke 6 is well known and generally understood. Those who insist on two categories of believers, however, often approach this passage with a need to reinterpret it in the light of their understanding of the Christian life.

Hodges sees the two builders—the one who builds on sand and the other who builds on rock—as two believers. One is a disciple, the other an average believer. Although neither account mentions the term "disciple" he feels it is necessary to introduce that idea as a distinct category of believer. He does so because the Lord likens one of the two men to one "who hears the sayings and does them" (Matt. 7:26; Luke 6:47). The idea of "doing" or performing for Christ as an expected spiritual instinct of the Christian is foreign to the nonlordship view. For Hodges the man who builds on sand is the Christian whose life has been wasted in carnal living and not used for the glory of God. The other man, according to his view, is the disciple who has committed his life in service to Christ as his Lord.[13] Hodges compares this parable to the "doers" and "hearers" of the Word in James 1, about which he says of a Christian: "If he was a hearer only, he was risking a colossal disaster. He was consigning his earthly experiences to tragic ruin."[14]

Hodges then speaks of the "hearing only" believer in contrast to the "hearing-doing" believers: "There it was again! The water and the food! The gift of God on the one hand, freely bestowed and eternally unfailing. And *on the other hand*, the call to discipleship, to do the will of God and to finish his work."[15] In other words, the average believer has the gift of life without works, while the disciple-believer desires to perform God's will.

It seems obvious that Hodges has missed the point for several reasons: First, as previously stated, faith is far more than intellectual assent and receiving of goods. It is a "believing into," a wholehearted loving trust of the one in whom faith is placed. The nonlordship view makes faith simply a hearing and forgetting.

Second, in its context this passage is part of an unmistakable progression. In Matthew 7:13 Christ calls His listeners to enter the narrow gate, as opposed to the wide gate to destruction. This speaks of entering salvation through the only Door, Christ (John 10), who is the only Way (John 14:6). Those who enter any other way are doomed to "destruction" (*apoleian*), a strong term signifying eternal punishment (cf. Rom. 9:22; Phil. 3:19; 2 Peter 2:1; 3:16). In these verses the "tragic ruin" (to use Hodges's phrase) is not the waste of Christian opportunity in fruitless living, but the destruction of life in hell.

In verses 15–20 the Lord warns that false prophets in sheep's clothing are everywhere seeking to mislead the believer. The way to identify false prophets, who are really wolves and not sheep, is by observing their fruit—their life pattern. The sheep are the Christians; the wolves or false prophets are not.

In verse 23 Christ banishes those who falsely claim His name: "I never knew you; depart from Me, you who practice lawlessness!" He uses "know" in the sense of "love," as in Genesis 4:1; Amos 3:2; Luke 1:34; and 1 Corinthians 8:3. Christ had never loved these people in the sense that He loves true believers. The subjects of this parable claim to be Christian, but they are not, as is evident by their not doing the will of the Father. They do *not* "enter the kingdom of heaven" (v. 21).

Third, since all these previous statements contrast the believer and the nonbeliever, it is natural for Jesus to tell how to become a true believer: by wisely building upon a sure foundation, or by truly trusting on Him. Christ is the true foundation for eternal life (1 Cor. 3:11; Eph. 2:20).

The contrast between the two builders is one of "hearing and not doing" versus "hearing and doing"

(Luke 6:47, 49). A person's "not doing" manifests the emptiness of his profession. The one who merely says, "Lord, Lord" and does not do what is commanded is not a true believer (Luke 6:46). The true believer is founded upon the Rock of Ages and performs with Christ's indwelling Spirit motivating him.

The Slothful Servant

The parables of the slothful servant in Matthew 25:14–30 and Luke 19:11–27 are thought to be two distinct parables.[16] They are similar enough, however, to be considered as teaching the same theme, as Pentecost and others agree.

A master leaves his slaves with varying amounts of money, which he entrusts them to use for his benefit. Two servants increase their entrustments, but the third does not. Upon the master's return he rewards the two faithful servants and punishes the slothful one.

Pentecost sees all of these men as believers. Two are disciples, worthy of reward, but the third is not. Pentecost explains: "This man not only lost his reward, he also lost the privilege of serving the master that had been originally entrusted to him. The misuse of discipleship will remove one from the enjoyment of its privileges."[17] He then compares the two parables and concludes that they teach discipleship as entailing an obligation that is not required of the average believer.[18]

That such an interpretation could be foisted upon the parable is remarkable for several reasons: First, the latter portion of the Olivet discourse (Matt. 24:36–25:46), in which this parable is found, concerns Christ's Second Advent. The Lord is illustrating the opposite conditions of men who will be found at the end of the world. The context is particularly interested in setting forth the difference between believers and unbelievers, not faithful believers and unfaithful believers.

In evidence of this, notice the following. (1) Christ speaks of the people in Noah's day who were destroyed, leaving only Noah and his family (Matt. 24:36–39). (2) The two women grinding (24:40–41) represent one saved and one lost—as Pentecost himself recognizes.[19] (3) The parable of the wicked servant contrasts the attitudes of the lost and the saved (24:45–51). The lost are assigned to judgment in "weeping and gnashing" pain (i.e., hell) among the hypocrites, such as the doomed Pharisees (Matt. 23:13–15). (4) According to Pentecost, the ten virgins picture the saved and the lost of Israel.[20] Certainly they do represent the saved and lost, though not just of Israel. (5) Following the parable, the judgment of the nations takes place (Matt. 25:31–46). In this judgment some are appointed to everlasting punishment (Matt. 25:41–46).

The entire discourse has the tone of judgment and blessing. The unsaved are consistently placed in stark contrast to the saved. It is therefore unnecessary to assume anything different about the parable of the slothful servant in the same context. The idea of discipleship as an additional, extraordinary commitment on the part of some believers is foreign to Matthew's thought. The one who is faithful and is rewarded is the believer; his reward is eternal life. The unfaithful man is the unbeliever, who is consigned to eternal destruction.

Second, the slothful servant's judgment (25:30)

strongly indicates condemnation: (1) His confinement is in darkness, which generally represents evil and judgment (cf. John 1:4–5, 6; 1 John 1:6; Eph. 5:11; 2 Peter 2:4). (2) The idea expressed by the phrase "weeping and gnashing of teeth" consistently indicates the torment of hell in Scripture (Matt. 13:42; 22:13; 24:51; Luke 13:28). The believer, in contrast, has no condemnation (Rom. 8:1).

Third, the slothful servant terribly misunderstands the master and morbidly fears him (25:24, 25). But in the genuine Christian's relationship to Christ, John says, "There is no fear in love; but perfect love casts out fear, because fear involves torment" (1 John 4:18).

Again, it cannot be reasonably maintained that this parable involves discipleship in the nonlordship sense of the term. The contrast is between the spiritual consistency of the saved and the idle neglect of the lost at Christ's Return.

Denying Self

Several passages speak of denying oneself and wholeheartedly following the Master. Matthew 16:24–27; Mark 8:34–38; and Luke 9:23–26 represent one discourse on this point. Since they are parallel accounts, for convenience sake we shall look mainly at Luke's passage.

> Then He said to them all, "If anyone desires to come after Me, let him deny himself, and take up his cross daily, and follow Me. For whoever desires to save his life will lose it, but whoever loses his life for My sake will save it. For what advantage is it to a man if he

gains the whole world, and is himself destroyed or lost? For whoever is ashamed of Me and of My words, of him the Son of Man will be ashamed when He comes in His own glory, and in His Father's, and of the holy angels." (Luke 9:23–26)

Bearing in mind Pentecost's definition of discipleship, notice how he interprets Luke's account of the "self-denial" discourse: "Christ said, 'If anyone who began as a curious believer and consequently called himself a disciple, as a result of exposure to my teaching is convinced that I am the Messiah, the Son of God, and will commit himself totally to me, that one becomes my disciple but not until then.'"[21]

Pentecost reasons from the intolerant religious attitude of the Jews toward Christ in His day. After discussing at length the extreme animosity of the Jewish nation toward Christ, he concludes that for one to become closely attached to Christ and His movement was tantamount to socio-religious suicide. The ostracism of such a person would entail estrangement from family, friends, and community. In short, it was a self–denial. Since many believers would not do this for fear of the people, Christ needed to call for extra commitment from among the believers.[22]

Nonlordship proponents commonly make this sharp class distinction among believers. Such a view is, however, untenable. First, although Pentecost's understanding of the Jewish animosity toward Christ is correct, we must recognize that for a Jew to believe in Christ *at all* meant socio-religious suicide. The Jews had agreed to put any man out of the synagogue who confessed that Jesus was the Christ (John 9:22; 12:42), not just those who lived close to Him and followed Him about the country. The blind man whom Jesus healed in John 9 had but a brief encounter with Christ and afterwards did not even know of Jesus' whereabouts (9:12). Nevertheless his confidence in Christ's goodness and ability (9:25, 30–33) led the Pharisees to call him a disciple (9:28) and to cast him out of the synagogue (9:34). They understood discipleship to be a supreme trust or belief in another—even if the disciple did not follow Christ about the countryside.

Thus this message, which was spoken to the "crowd" (Mark 8:34, NIV), was given so that those gathered before Him would realize what believing in Him entails. Christ looked at the crowd and said, "If anyone desires to come after Me. . . ." He did not ask believers if they wished to go on to a higher level of commitment. This was an evangelistic message. Great crowds flocked to Him throughout His ministry, but when He began calling for their allegiance in a true faith commitment, the test was on. Here is where those who followed Him merely for physical benefit or wonderment were separated from those who followed Him because He had "the words of life." Many would follow Him as long as they could see the miracles and received no resistance from their fellow countrymen. These were merely professing believers who lacked genuine faith (note John 2:23–25; 6:60–69).

Second, in the "denial" passages Jesus says that if anyone desires (Greek: *thelo*) to come to Him, he must be willing to do three things: deny himself, take up his cross daily, and follow Him. Each of these is a different aspect of a life of true faith and trust in Christ. People with a desire must act upon that desire, not in empty profession, but in a profession girded with commitment.

Here "to deny" is from the Greek *arneomai,* which means to "disregard oneself." It is the same verb used of Moses' disregarding of his high and privileged position as the adopted son of Pharaoh's daughter for the cause of God (Heb. 11:24). It is paralleled in the verse with "let him follow me." This following is expressed by the verb *akoloutheo,* which is used in John 10:27 where Jesus asserts: "My sheep hear My voice . . . and they follow Me." Jesus pointedly says that His sheep both hear *and* follow Him. A person who truly receives Christ as Savior is in effect denying himself—considering himself and his wants as nothing and Christ as everything.

Jesus is here warning that true faith in Him is not, as J. C. Ryle put it, "putting a man in an armchair and taking him easily to heaven. It is the beginning of a mighty conflict."[23] Christian faith results in Christian *life,* and Christian life is, by its very nature, in conflict with the world and self. This is not to say that in order to be a Christian one has to perform certain prerequisite, meritorious works. It simply affirms that to follow Christ for eternal life means having an attitude of self-denial and looking in trust and hope, not to self, but to Christ as Lord.

Third, in Luke 9:23 the initial imperative statements calling for self-denial, cross-bearing, and following Christ are the message Christ preached, while verses 24–26 are the reasons for that message, which indicate it is a matter of spiritual life or death.

The conjunction "for" (*gar*) connects each of the following phrases in verses 24–26. It is used in the common sense of expressing reason. Thus, the call of Christ in verse 23 has attached to it warnings of the consequences of refusing to heed His message. To refuse His call—to resist self-denial, cross-bearing, and following Him—is serious. Such refusal is equivalent to attempting to save your own soul only to lose it (v. 24), seeking to gain the whole world only to lose your soul (v. 25), and being ashamed of Christ only to have Christ be ashamed of you in return (v. 26).

The obvious contrast in these statements is between temporary physical gain and permanent spiritual gain. The eternal destiny of the soul is far more important than gaining present material satisfaction in one's temporal existence.

This passage closely parallels Mark 9:44–48 in thought. Mark says Jesus taught that it is better to live the present life with only one hand, foot, or eye than having both and living for self, only to be cast into hell at death. Self-denial—the heart attitude and willingness inherent in trusting in Christ—enables the believer to withstand the scoldings, persecution, and suffering the world brings him. Even though he will fail from time to time and never reaches perfection in this life, no true believer renounces from his heart his trust in Christ and lives in opposition to Him. Trust in Christ is the natural outgrowth of accepting Him as Lord, and it perseveres under God's providential care.

The rich young ruler in Matthew 19:16–26 had confidence in himself (v. 20) and was not willing to turn the control of his life and his riches over to Christ (v. 22). His self-sufficiency ruled his life. Had he come to Christ in absolute, obedient trust, he could have laid hold of eternal life. Instead he went away sorrowing (v. 22), longing to gain the world rather than deny himself and follow Christ.

Pentecost's notion that Luke 9:23–27 refers to the believer and "is a contest for mastery, a contest for the right to rule" simply does not fit the facts.[24] Christ is warning careless onlookers that He means business when He asks for a person's trust. He commands everyone to love Him with all one's heart, soul, mind, and strength (Mark 12:33).

Conclusion

Many other discipleship passages could be studied in addition to these surveyed. This chapter has simply provided a brief demonstration of the error involved in popular notions of discipleship.

Jesus' discipleship discourses served a two-fold purpose: to discourage thoughtless onlookers by dispelling their false hopes, and to bring about true conversion. Those who heard only outwardly would not turn to Him and be forgiven (Mark 4:12). But those whose hearts the Holy Spirit opened to the Truth would turn from their sins and cast themselves before Christ in faith.

Discipleship passages illustrate what being a believer really means. They do not teach a higher life based upon some second decision for Christ. The true Christian is distinguished by his self-denying love for God and other Christians. "By this all will know that you are My disciples, if you have love for one another" (John 13:35). Most nonlordship proponents do not see this as the normal Christian behavior. Instead, as Pentecost says, this love is the "badge of discipleship," by which he means higher Christian living.[25] But the apostle John clearly and emphatically teaches: "He who does not love does not know God, for God is love. . . . If someone says, 'I love God,' and hates his brother, he is a liar" (1 John 4:8, 20).

Every true believer is a disciple because he has been redeemed from his sin by Christ in order to serve God.

Notes

1. Charles Ryrie, in Zane C. Hodges, *The Hungry Inherit* (Chicago: Moody, 1972), 7. Emphasis mine.

2. J. Dwight Pentecost, *Design for Discipleship* (Grand Rapids: Zondervan, 1971), 11.

3. Ibid., 14.

4. Zane C. Hodges, *Absolutely Free!* (Grand Rapids: Zondervan, 1989), 87.

5. John R. W. Stott, *Basic Christianity* (Grand Rapids: Eerdmans, 1958), 109.

6. John F. MacArthur, Jr., *The Gospel According to Jesus* (Grand Rapids: Zondervan, 1988), 196, 197.

7. W. Baur, *A Greek-English Lexicon of the New Testament*, trans. and rev. W. F. Arndt and F. W. Gingrich (Chicago: University of Chicago, 1957), 487.

8. Pentecost, *Design for Discipleship*, 14. Roy B. Zuck, "Cheap Grace?," *Kindred Spirit* (Summer 1981), 6.

9. Baur, *Greek-English Lexicon*, 487.

10. A. T. Robertson, *A Harmony of the Gospels* (New York: Harper and Row, 1950), 249–50.

11. For a detailed study of the implications of the Great Commission, see my *The Greatness of the Great Commission:*

The Christian Enterprise in a Fallen World (Tyler, Tex.: Institute for Christian Economics, 1990).

12. Everett F. Harrison, "Must Christ Be Lord to Be Savior—No!," *Eternity*, 10 (Sept. 1959): 14.

13. Hodges, *The Hungry Inherit*, 89–90.

14. Ibid., 91–92.

15. Ibid., emphasis mine.

16. Richard C. Trench, *Notes on the Miracles and Parables of Our Lord* (Old Tappen, N.J.: Revell, rep. 1953), 2:271.

17. Pentecost, *Design for Discipleship*, 127. See also Warren W. Wiersbe, *The Bible Exposition Commentary* (Wheaton, Ill.: Victor, 1989), 1:92.

18. Ibid., 124.

19. J. Dwight Pentecost, *Things to Come* (Grand Rapids: Zondervan, 1958), 162.

20. Ibid., 414.

21. Pentecost, *Design for Discipleship*, 18. See also Wiersbe, *The Bible Exposition Commentary*, 1:207.

22. Ibid., 35–36.

23. J. C. Ryle, *Holiness* (Greenwood, S.C.: Attic, rep. 1956), 69.

24. Pentecost, *Design for Discipleship*, 41.

25. Ibid., 60.

6

Preaching the Lord of Salvation

My sheep hear My voice, and I know them, and they follow Me. And I give them eternal life, and they shall never perish; neither shall anyone snatch them out of My hand. (John 10:27–28)

The presentation of Christ in modern evangelism leaves much to be desired. As a result, Christian leaders are too often mired in efforts to motivate fruitless professing Christians. Very often these merely professing Christians end up in leadership positions themselves. Perhaps that is why nonlordship advocates respond to lordship arguments with the plea, "Where is there room for carnal Christians?"[1] MacArthur responds: "The cheap grace and easy faith of a distorted gospel are ruining the purity of the church. The softening of the New Testament message has brought with it a putrefying inclusivism that in effect sees almost any kind of positive response to Jesus as tantamount to saving faith."[2]

Evangelism Deficiencies

If the glory of God were the motivating force in soul-winning, Christians would not have to be taught to be hypocritical in their witnessing. One evangelism training manual instructs the witness: "Every time you go in a home, brag on something. We live in a selfish world. It is good to say, 'You sure have a nice suit,' or 'Isn't that a precious child?' Make it a habit. Develop it inwardly."[3]

If modern evangelism had more confidence in the work of the Holy Spirit, it would be more faithful to content than to form. It is said of Dwight L. Moody, an early developer of modern evangelistic methodology, that he "completed the reduction of evangelism to a matter of technique and personality."[4] A more recent evangelist encourages the use of the piano over the organ in evangelistic meetings because the organ "is not a percussion instrument. The air blowing into one giant tube and then another does not make the instant staccato beginning of a note as does the piano," thus losing the urgency of the message.[5] All of this is important because "evangelism is an atmosphere. Music can help create this atmosphere."[6]

If the hateful offensiveness of sin before God were more carefully preached, and repentance from that sinful state consistently urged, there would be fewer "carnal" Christians with which to deal. It actually seems as if sin, according to some (not all) nonlordship spokesmen is of very little consequence. R. B. Thieme is one who seems incognizant of the true offensiveness of sin. He teaches what he terms the "rebound technique" of confession of sin. Before each Bible study he conducts, he instructs his followers to "confess" their sins by simply naming them and forgetting them:

> In the preparation for our study of the Word of God this evening the next few minutes are devoted to silent prayer. Our objective is to prepare ourselves in the usual manner. . . . The usual manner being the only way, is the "rebound technique." A totally nonmeritorious function on our part. The only thing we do is the sinning. The naming of the sin is totally without any human merit whatever. How you feel about it is *not of any consequence to God;* just *simply name your sin* and you are forgiven and at the same time you are filled with the Spirit.[7]

Lordship advocates teach that believing in Christ and resolving to obey Him are not two acts but one. When Christ is preached, He should be presented in His whole person—as Lord and Savior. The resulting life of obedience to Christ is the true test of the validity of the initial act of faith. Nonlordship doctrine boldly claims that conversion to Christ in salvation involves "no spiritual commitment whatsoever."[8] Many "Christians" today sadly fail the test, for they have simply not counted the cost. They have instead attempted to place one hand in Christ's in hope of eternal glory, while reserving the other for self and carnal pleasure.

Lordship Basics

The lordship presentation of Christ is grounded on four basic truths:

First, true faith in Christ inseparably binds one to the person of Christ. This spiritual binding must be understood as real, vital, and effective, not as a simply apprehension of facts about Christ. It involves a determined commitment of oneself to Him.

Second, repentance is not an outdated message for another dispensation. The resolve to forsake sin in turning to Christ is essential today. Christ does not save a man *in* his sins, but *from* them. The awfulness of sin is impressed upon the person by the Holy Spirit, which results in this heartfelt change of mind about it. This results in a humble turning to Christ from sin and self.

Third, the Savior is none other than Jesus Christ the Lord. An essential attribute of His divine character is sovereignty. His position as Son of Man was appointed for Him by the Father in order ultimately to give Him power, dominion, and rule in the affairs of men. A person cannot truly turn to the Lord and continue blithely as before in the sin that separated him from God in the first place. The unregenerate sinner is lord of his own life; Christ is Lord of the believer's life.

Fourth, Jesus' call to discipleship is an exhortation for men totally to trust Him as the only means of eternal life. Certainly no works are prerequisite for salvation (2 Tim. 1:9; Eph. 2:8–9), but neither is true salvation devoid of work (James 2). The "armchair Christian" has no reason for assurance of eternal bliss. Turning to the Lord in repentance and faith is costly and demanding, not cheap and easy.

The Nature of Salvation

A. W. Pink has rightly stated, "Salvation is a supernatural work which produces supernatural effects."[9] The dog returns to his vomit and the swine to the mud, but the believer stands in a new relationship to God (2 Peter 2:22; 2 Cor. 5:17). The Scriptures say of the believer that he is chosen to be holy (Eph. 1:4), to be obedient (1 Peter 1:2), and to bear fruit (John 15:16). He is ordained to do good works (Eph. 2:10). He follows Christ (John 10:27). Christ died for him in order to redeem him from iniquity (Titus 2:14), to move him to live in righteousness (1 Peter 2:24), and to cause him to serve without fear in holiness and righteousness (Luke 1:74–75). He is predestined to be conformed to the image of Christ (Rom. 8:29). That conforming to Christ begins with the new birth and is ultimately perfected in heaven. The believer is described as a "called, chosen, and *faithful*" person (Rev. 17:14).

Paul sternly warns professing believers, "Examine yourselves as to whether you are in the faith. Prove yourselves" (2 Cor. 13:5). John teaches, "No one who is born of God practices sin" (1 John 3:9, NASB). James says, "Faith without works is dead" (James 2:20). Faith is living, productive, and fruitful. That does not imply perfectionism, eradicationism (the eradication of the sin nature), synergism (redemption by the aid of man), or autosoterism (self-salvation). The lordship view of discipleship is essentially the same as the nonlordship view, except that *all* believers are considered disciples.

People are saved by God's sovereign grace. That grace is channeled into the heart through repentant faith in the Lord Jesus Christ. The inclination and ability to believe is purely a product of God's efficacious grace.[10] The natural man does not have the power to believe: "No one can come to Me, unless it has been granted him by My Father" (John 6:65b). We who would evangelize must realize that "unless one is born again, he cannot see the kingdom of God" (John 3:3), because "the natural man does not receive the things of the Spirit of God: for they are foolishness to him; nor can he know them, because they are spiritually discerned" (1 Cor. 2:14).

So also the obedient Christian's life—though it has its ups and downs—is purely by God's grace, which produces perseverance. Good works are the natural fruit of regeneration, contrary to the nonlordship view, which insists that works are not natural for the believer (see appendix).

There are good reasons to expect the truly redeemed to yield fruit over the long run. Their salvation is the result of supernatural operations, not unaided belief. Nor do they receive a mere addition to their lives. True salvation involves a change in one's life.

The Bible says the Christian is blessed with "every spiritual blessing" (Eph. 1:3). Indeed, the Lord's "divine power has given to us all things that pertain to life and godliness" (2 Peter 1:3a). The true Christian is under the power of grace, not of external law; consequently "sin shall not have dominion over you, for you are not under law but under grace" (Rom. 6:14).

The convert to Christ is indwelled by the Holy Spirit of God (Rom. 8:10; Gal. 2:20). He has died to sin (Rom. 6:2, 4, 6, 14; Gal. 1:4; Col. 1:12–13), having been resurrected from spiritual death to spiritual life: "For as the Father raises the dead and gives life to them, even so the Son gives life to whom He will" (John 5:21). Thus, he "has passed from death into life" (John 5:24b; cp. Rom. 6:4–9; Col. 2:13). Because of this the Christian has a new heart (Ezek. 11:19; 36:26) and is a "new man" (Eph. 4:22–24; Col. 3:9–10), a "new creation" (2 Cor. 5:17; Gal. 6:15; Eph. 2:10). God's power works within the Christian (Eph. 1:19; Titus 3:5) as Christ intercedes for him (Rom. 8:34; Heb. 7:25).

An illustration of the all-too-frequent trifling of the gospel in nonlordship preaching can be seen in the following evangelistic training. One pastor of a large church teaches a soul-winning course that includes such statements as: "God is hard up and He will even use you." "If you have trouble raising your money [for the church], just get some sinners converted." "I tell my preacher boys in my church, 'If you go to a church where they are about to vote you out, kick you out, go out and win enough folks to carry the vote right quick."[11] The implication is not only that a person's salvation depends on someone else's work, but also that a lost sinner is of little more value than one more vote to keep the pastor. Are these "converts" being presented Christ in the biblical sense?

Of course, not all nonlordship advocates would utter such things. Yet some, tempted by the implications of nonlordship doctrine, actually do practice such tactics.

Often this method is defended on the ground that it is effective and results in numerous confessions and therefore must be the work of God. But that is faulty logic, as well as bad theology. Even the heretical Mormon Church claims God's blessing upon its amazing success. Past Mormon president LeGrand Richards has confidently declared regarding the Church of Jesus Christ of Latter-day Saints: "Is there any other organization to compare with it in all the world? This could not be the work of man—it must be the work of God."[12] Such ethical reasoning is derived from the Jesuit intentionalistic philosophy, which teaches that the end justifies the means. It is totally unscriptural, as seen in such passages as Romans 3:8 and 6:1, 2. Moses received water from the rock when he disobediently struck it, but that did not prove his action right (Num. 20:7–13).

Conclusion

The story is told of an accidental splicing of two advertisements in a newspaper. Somehow a car dealer's ad was merged with a church advertisement. The resulting ad read: "We preach Jesus Christ at the lowest price in years." The current trend is to preach Jesus Christ "at the lowest price," confusing free grace with freedom to disregard the rightful demands of Christ's lordship. Such is the natural consequence of nonlordship theology.

Scripture preaches salvation in none other than the Lord of Lords and King of Kings.

Notes

1. Charles C. Ryrie, *Balancing the Christian Life* (Chicago: Moody, 1969), 170.

2. John F. MacArthur, Jr., *The Gospel According to Jesus* (Grand Rapids: Zondervan, 1988), 37.

3. Jack Hyles, *Let's Go Soul Winning!* (Murfreesboro, Tenn.: Sword of the Lord, 1962), 22.

4. Cited in George Dollar, *A History of Fundamentalism in America* (Greenville, S.C.: Bob Jones, 1973), 78.

5. John R. Rice, *Why Our Churches Do Not Win Souls* (Murfreesboro, Tenn.: Sword of the Lord, 1966), 120–21.

6. Jack Hyles, *The Hyles Church Manual* (Murfreesboro, Tenn.: Sword of the Lord, 1968), 190.

7. R. B. Thieme, "Ephesians," Cassette tape # 413–029 (Houston, TX: Berachah Church, June 13, 1975). Emphasis mine.

8. Zane C. Hodges, *The Gospel Under Siege* (Dallas: Redencion Viva, 1981), 14.

9. Arthur W. Pink, *The Saint's Perseverance* (MacDill A.F.B., Fla.: Tyndale Bible Society, n.d.), 8.

10. John Murray, *Redemption: Accomplished and Applied* (Grand Rapids: Eerdmans, 1965), chaps. 1–3.

11. Hyles, *Let's Go Soul Winning!*, 8, 6, 7.

12. LeGrand Richards, *A Marvelous Work and Wonder* (Salt Lake City, Utah: Deseret, 1958), 168.

Appendix:

The Higher Life Movement

As mentioned in chapter 1 the nonlordship view has two main factions, which presumably have their differences. For example, nonlordship advocate L. S. Chafer himself sees no scriptural basis for the Higher Life movement. But when one examines the doctrines espoused by the two nonlordship camps, it becomes apparent that they are virtually indistinguishable.

The quotations below demonstrate the similarity between the two branches. The problem with both, as Warfield has noted, is that "we cannot divide Jesus and have Him as our righteousness while not at the same time having Him as our sanctification."[1]

The Higher Life Camp

In the divine order God's working depends upon our co-operation. . . . Just as a potter, however skillful, cannot make a beautiful vessel out of a lump of clay that is never put into his hands, so neither can God make out of me a vessel unto His honor, unless I put myself into His hands.

—Hannah Whitehall Smith[2]

By a definite voluntary act of the will the believer must choose Christ as the new Master and yield himself to Him as Lord.

—Ruth Paxson[3]

The Discipleship Camp

Very often these days dedication is mixed up with salvation. . . . Simply stated, dedication concerns whether I will direct my life or whether Christ will.

—Charles C. Ryrie[4]

Until you present yourself in a definite act to Jesus Christ, you are not a disciple.

—J. Dwight Pentecost[5]

The Higher Life Camp

Just as the death of Christ *for* you is only *potential* until by a deliberate and voluntary *act* of faith you appropriate its efficacy for your redemption, so *your* death *with* Christ is only potential unless by a deliberate and voluntary *attitude* of faith you appropriate its efficacy for your sanctification—enabling God to put you once more to that intelligent use for which He created you, and for which Christ has now redeemed you.

—Major Ian W. Thomas[6]

The Discipleship Camp

In speaking of being ordained to good works, Chafer notes:

They are none other than those good works which have been before ordained for each believer. Such "good works" can be discovered . . . only as the life is wholly yielded to God.

—L. S. Chafer[7]

A believer becomes a disciple of Jesus Christ when he submits to the authority of Christ's word and acknowledges Christ's right to rule over him. . . . An ox does not accidently slip into a yoke. He has to submit to it.

—J. Dwight Pentecost[8]

Bondslaves are by nature rebels. And we are rebels against the authority of Christ; we *delight* to superimpose our will against the will of Christ. . . .

—J. Dwight Pentecost[9]

Notes

1. Benjamin B. Warfield, *Perfectionism* (Nutley, N.J.: Presbyterian and Reformed, 1958), 258.

2. Cited in ibid., 291.

3. Ruth Paxson, *Life on the Highest Plane* (Chicago: Bible Colportage, 1941), 2:123.

4. Charles C. Ryrie, *Balancing the Christian Life* (Chicago: Moody, 1969), 78.

5. J. Dwight Pentecost, *Design for Discipleship* (Grand Rapids: Zondervan, 1971), 38.

6. Ian W. Thomas, *The Mystery of Godliness* (Grand Rapids: Zondervan, 1964), 137.

7. L. S. Chafer, *Grace* (Grand Rapids: Zondervan, 1922), 25.

8. Pentecost, *Design for Discipleship*, 29.

9. Ibid., 41.

Index of Scripture

Index of Scripture